THE BAYEUX TAPESTRY

THE BAYEVX TAPESTRY

THE COMPLETE TAPESTRY
IN COLOUR
WITH INTRODUCTION, DESCRIPTION
AND COMMENTARY BY
DAVID M. WILSON

Director of the British Museum

THAMES AND HUDSON

To Simon and Kate

Note on the Photography

The colour pictures of the Tapestry are reproduced with the special authorization of the Town of Bayeux. The scale of reproduction is approximately fifty-four per cent of the original. The photographs were taken by natural light when the Tapestry was removed from its case. When on public display, it is viewed through glass which slightly changes the colour values.

Additional Photographic Acknowledgments

1 Archives Photographiques, Paris. This is part of a complete photographic record of the back of the Tapestry (No. 58 from a total of 82 negatives) made by the Ministère de la Culture (Direction du Patrimoine) during the scientific examination that took place 1982–3. 2 Courtauld Institute, London. 3 Universitetets Oldsaksamling, Oslo. 4 Tiegens Fotoatelier A/S, Oslo. 5 Winchester Excavations Committee. 6 British Library, London. 7 British Museum, London. 8 Courtauld Institute, London. 9,10 British Library, London. 11 Courtauld Institute, London. 12 Universitetets Oldsaksamling, Oslo. 13 York Archaeological Trust. 14 A.F. Kersting. 15 British Library, London. 16 From D. Hejdová, 'Přilba Zvaná "Svatováclavská"', *Sborník Národního Muzea v Praze*, Ser. A, xviii (1964). Photo: Josef Ehm. 17 Germanisches Nationalmuseum, Nuremberg. 18,19 British Museum, London.

Text © 1985 Sir David Wilson
Illustrations and layout © 1985 Thames and Hudson Ltd, London
Map: Hanni Bailey

Printed and bound in Japan

CONTENTS

———◆———

———◆———

Foreword

THE BAYEUX TAPESTRY . . . I discovered it long ago. I was twelve years old, the age when one grows out of childhood into adolescence, and my craving for knowledge, for discovery, knew no bounds. I read everything, voraciously. I knew the great Norman writers, Corneille, Flaubert, Maupassant, Barbey d'Aurevilly. I was enthralled by a History of Normandy which celebrated the exalted deeds of the rough northmen of the past. The story of Rollo, who lifted the king of France's foot to his lips rather than submit to bow his head, filled me with enthusiasm. I knew the principal facts of the life of William, bastard, duke and king – and I knew that in a city called Bayeux there was a magnificent cathedral which held in its Treasury – from whence it emerged to be displayed in the chancel on the major feast days – a Tapestry which told in pictures the story of the conquest of England.

I was a Norman from the other end of the province, beyond the Seine, and had travelled little; for me the existence of this remote city took on something of a mythical quality.

I had just taken my primary school certificate, and, as a reward, my parents drove me across to Mont St Michel – quite an expedition at that time, in the 1930s, when many roads were still rocky or cobbled tracks. We had planned to travel by way of Bayeux and go to Mass on Assumption Day, 15 August. The bishop officiated, attended by his Chapter; it was a Pontifical High Mass. Magnificent! But where was the Tapestry? Nowhere to be seen. The service over, I dragged my parents off to explore the cathedral. Nothing. I caught sight of a verger in full dress, blazing with purple and gold, mustachioed like an ancient Gaul, with stockings *à la française* and halberd in hand; and I overcame my shyness sufficiently to approach him. 'Excuse me, Monsieur, but why is the Tapestry not on show today?' 'It is not shown in the cathedral, hasn't been for years. You have to go to the library for that, young man. Go out by the side door and it's just opposite.'

'Can't be done,' my father broke in, 'we haven't got time.'

My world collapsed in bitter tears of disappointment. The verger, armed with all the majesty of his calling, turned on my father. 'Monsieur, it is just not possible to leave Bayeux without seeing the Tapestry.' My father gave in, and we went into the Deanery building, which housed the Tapestry.

Upstairs, in a room which seemed to me immense, there was the masterpiece, all seventy metres of it, and I looked – and found myself drawn into the Tapestry, utterly absorbed by this legacy of the distant past.

In my imagination, I moved among the characters, identifying myself now with one, now with another in turn. I was King Edward, and then, just as vividly, I became

Harold. I came ashore on the coast of Ponthieu; I was both Count Guy and his prisoner; I was William, then Harold again – and then I was one of those he saved from drowning at the crossing of the Couesnon. I was William again to receive the keys of Dinan on the tip of a lance; and I was Harold once more, swearing his oath upon the holy relics. Then came the sea voyage, the landing, and the Battle of Hastings. Once more I was both William and Harold; the arrow was in my eye; I was the linen of the canvas and the wool of the embroidery.

I saw the Tapestry again twenty years later, but could not recapture the overwhelming emotions of my twelve-year-old self. The setting and the presentation seemed to me unworthy of the treasure which they ostensibly served.

It is these experiences – these two encounters twenty years apart – that explain why, when I became mayor of Bayeux, I was determined to give the Tapestry the setting it merits, while at the same time improving the conditions of its conservation.

The Bayeux Tapestry is now in the former Grand Seminaire, a large building whose sober, well-proportioned late seventeenth-century architecture admirably sets off its simple but intensely vital lines, and its warm and living colours.

The room which now houses it promotes a contemplative state of mind. A muted calm prevails along all seventy metres of the U-shaped gallery, and the skilfully controlled lighting, all of which comes from inside the showcase, seems to emanate from the Tapestry itself. The dimly seen wooden roof, in the shape of an upturned ship's keel, almost subliminally stresses the important role played by William's ships, and the crucial part he himself played in the course of history.

William, Duke of Normandy, came to England as a conqueror; but since then a network of historical ties, woven of quarrels and reconciliations, has come into being to unite Normans and Anglo-Saxons. We have not forgotten, after nine hundred years, the truth recalled by that simple phrase carved in stone in the war cemetery at Bayeux where the young British soldiers lie: *Nos a Gulielmo victi victoris patriam liberavimus* (We, who were conquered by William, have freed the land of our conqueror).

Thanks are due to the English publishers, Thames and Hudson, who, by virtue of the exceptional quality of their work in this volume, have made it possible to keep in one's possession – or to discover for the first time – for the delectation of the soul and of the heart, the beauty of this masterpiece which is a witness to our common history.

JEAN LE CARPENTIER
Conseiller Général
Maire de Bayeux

Preface

THE BAYEUX TAPESTRY is one of the most numinous monuments of European history. The opportunity to publish a full and accurate colour reproduction of it is a challenge and an opportunity for which any medievalist would give his eye teeth. I hope that I have lived up to the challenge. The glory of the book lies in the pictures that were taken by Clichés Ville de Bayeux at the time of the rehanging of the Tapestry in 1982–3. This rehanging has prompted a more thorough examination of some aspects of the story told by the Tapestry, and I have been able to provide more up-to-date comparative material. Apart from this, and two or three new ideas, the text is a work of synthesis. The foundations laid by previous scholars still stand, and I hope that the book will become a worthy successor to de Montfaucon, Stothard, Fowke and Stenton as a source for seeing and appreciating the quality and detail of this unique historical monument.

Many people have helped me during the writing of this book. First my debt must be expressed to the Mayor of Bayeux, M. Jean Le Carpentier, for permission to publish his city's most precious monument. To his name must be added those of Mme Michèle Coïc, Bibliothécaire-Conservateur, and Mme Liliane Bouillon, Directrice, who were both most generous of their time and help during my physical examination of the hanging. I am grateful also to M. M. Charpillon, Sous-Directeur des Monuments Historiques of the French Ministry of Culture, and to his colleagues M. Macé de Lépinay and Mlle Bédat for help and information concerning the rehanging of the Tapestry and for permission to publish fig. 1 before the definitive report on the scientific work associated with the new display is published. I am grateful to many colleagues in the British Museum for help and advice, but particularly to Leslie Webster, who read most of a very messy draft manuscript, to Marjorie Caygill, best of assistants, for her final typing, and to Linda Brooks for all her help.

I must also thank the following for advice (not always taken, but certainly appreciated): Janet Backhouse, Allen Brown, Helen Clarke, Wendy Davies, Anne C. Edmonds, Bob Farrell, Chris Fell, Gillian Fellows-Jensen, Richard Gem, Signe Horn Fuglesang, Marta Hoffmann, Michael Lapidge, Elisabeth Okasha, Ray Page, Else Roesdahl, Holger Schmidt, Zdenék Smetánka, Eva Wilson, Simon Wilson, Elisabeth Zadora-Rio and George Zarnecki.

DAVID M. WILSON
The British Museum
March 1985

Introduction: A Work of Art and an Historical Document

COUNT WILLIAM came from Normandy into Pevensey on the eve of Michaelmas, and as soon as his men were able they constructed a fortification at the market of Hastings. This was told to King Harold and he then collected a large army and met William at the old apple tree, and William came upon him unexpectedly before his army was drawn up. Nevertheless, the king fought very hard with him together with the men who would stand by him, and there were many slain on either side. King Harold was killed there, and Earl Leofwine his brother, and Earl Gyrth his brother, and many good men, and the Frenchmen had possession of the field, as God granted to them for the people's sins.[1]

This laconic entry in the Anglo-Saxon Chronicle is the only contemporary account in the English language of one of the most dramatic events in the country's history. All other sources are in Latin, most tell the story from the Norman side; but the most interesting and one of the most reliable is the unique embroidery known as the Bayeux Tapestry which tells of the events which lead up to the Norman Conquest and of the Battle of Hastings itself in text and picture. It is presented with lively imagination and an originality which still teases the eye and adds enlightenment to the most traumatic event in English history. A running text in simple Latin identifies the various scenes.

The story is told in a manner that is not always easy to understand. Only a few years after William the Conqueror's assumption of the English crown many different versions were being recounted. That told in the Tapestry is perhaps the most coherent (although not necessarily the most reliable). But whatever its puzzles, whatever its purpose, its lively portrayal of an historic event brings out the superlatives in practically every modern writer who has discussed it.

The purpose of this book is to produce a complete colour reproduction of the Tapestry to the highest present-day standards and to summarize the state of knowledge concerning it. The book is avowedly synthetic, particularly as the notes and record photographs taken by the Sous-Direction des Monuments Historiques at the time of the re-hanging in 1982 have not yet been made publicly available. It is to be emphasized that the Tapestry as seen today has been much repaired over the centuries, particularly at both ends, that it is almost certain that the final scene is missing and that anyone who examines the original will see obvious repairs and reconstructions throughout.

In 1819 Charles Stothard delivered a careful set of drawings of the Bayeux Tapestry to the Society of Antiquaries of London and wrote:

The work in some parts of the Tapestry was destroyed, but more particularly where the subject draws towards a conclusion. The traces of the design only existing by means of the holes where the needles had passed. On attentively examining the traces thus left I found that in many places minute particles of the different coloured threads were still retained . . .[2]

The repairs carried out on the Tapestry may be instanced in the very first scene, where only two letters of the inscription recording the identity of King Edward appear in the earliest published engraving.[3] Yet as it appears now on the photograph (pl. 1) and in the original it looks convincing, as do other repairs which we know to have taken place since the extremely competent engraving by Sansonetti was published in 1838.[4] As with all historical sources, then, the Tapestry has to be used critically and with circumspection; but generally both the text and the pictures are correct, restorations are easily identified and major doubts as to later reconstructions are rare.

Description

The Tapestry is not *sensu strictu* a tapestry, but an embroidered strip of linen (made up of eight conjoined strips of different lengths), about 68.38 m long, and varying between 45.7 and 53.6 cm high (measurements taken after it had been remounted in 1983[5]). The Tapestry was originally longer, but (as has been pointed out) the end is damaged and incomplete. The seven joins in the Tapestry are apparently original and are almost invisible; in one place (pl. 15) the embroidered upper border is out of alignment, showing that in this case the pieces of linen were joined after the embroidery was completed. The linen seems originally to have had an off-white tone, and now has an off-white to greyish colour and is often stained by wax or iron salts. It is of a relatively fine tabby weave – 18 or 19 warp and weft threads per centimetre.[6] The embroidery is carried out in coloured wools in laid and couched work defined by stem or outline stitch; the same stitch was used for all linear elements and the lettering. Similar stitches are used to add detail or three-dimensional effect to the figures or objects portrayed.[7] No trace apparently remains on the Tapestry of any lines of construction or of any cartoon, although a preliminary drawing almost certainly existed and must have been transferred in some form to the linen base. The Anglo-Saxon artist would be familiar from manuscripts and sculpture with the methods of laying out a design, whether it was transferred from one medium to another, as with sculpture, or laid out on the base material itself, as in the manuscripts.[8]

Five principal colours were used: terracotta, blue-green, an old gold colour, olive green and blue; and two other colours can also be identified – a dark blue or black (which is used fairly consistently as far as the beginning of pl. 48, but then must have run out) and a sage green. Many of the later repairs are carried out mainly in a light yellow, orange and light greens. The outline is executed in all these colours. The conservators of 1983 were struck by the fact that the colours on the back of the tapestry were of almost the same tone as those on the front; there had been little or no fading. It should, however, be pointed out to the modern visitor to Bayeux that some of the brilliance of the colours is lost by the need to keep the light-levels low and by the necessary presence of security glass in front of the hanging. Because of the thickness of the wool and the manner of stitching, the surface is a mass of light and shade which gives a lively feeling to the embroidery and sometimes makes it difficult to be precise in a description of the colour of a particular feature.

The colours are not used naturalistically; a horse, for example, may be blue or buff and its musculature can be expressed in yellow or blue. The horses' legs and hooves are often of different, quite arbitrary, colours. Faces and hands of human figures are executed in outline only and no attempt is made to represent flesh tones; the same is true where any naked or partly naked human body is shown. In places (e.g. some of the upper planks in pls. 35–36) recent repairs can be seen where the colour is out of tone; a particularly popular colour used by the nineteenth-century restorers was a rather sickly yellow (e.g. in some of the thin lines of the comet in pl. 32). Despite the unnaturalistic colouring and the apparent slight element of caricature in the draughtsmanship, the massed colours and lively outlines are articulated with skill in an almost painterly fashion to give a bold impression with no hint of crudity or even naivety. It is for this reason that it is important to see the whole hanging in colour reproduction, for only thus can one understand the quality of the artist's imagination. Added to the technical quality, the spatial sense shown by the designer, together with his sense of mass, gives a tension and sense of movement which make the Tapestry an imaginative masterpiece.

The story is framed between borders at the top and bottom, as well as at the beginning (the end is missing). The borders are not, however, used throughout the length of the Tapestry: very occasionally, at moments of heightened tension or importance (e.g. pls. 31–35 and 40–43), the main scene takes over at least the upper border. With few exceptions the story is told in consecutive order of the events as they happened and the figures of the principal actors appear several times, although there is little attempt at accurate or differentiated portrayal. (A rare example of differentiation of an individual character is the representation of Edward the Confessor as a bearded, elderly man.) The borders are sometimes ornamental; sometimes they represent fables; sometimes they are used to portray a sub-plot and even possibly to foreshadow future events. Towards the end of the Tapestry, where the Battle of Hastings is depicted, the lower border is used to portray companies of archers, the dead and maimed, and the looting of bodies.

Within the canons and capabilities of contemporary art a remarkable naturalism is achieved. Certain artistic clichés are used, but they are rather grand ones – the representation of the interior of a house, for example, is rendered in a particularly conventionalized fashion. The Tapestry is an entirely competent piece of work in design, representation and execution. Furthermore, it presents a remarkable uniformity of style throughout its length. It was clearly designed (and its production supervised) by a single artist who based his interpretation of the historical events he portrayed on both written and oral sources. The designer may also have written the text, but certain inconsistencies make it difficult to state with any certainty that this was indeed the case. There is no loss of control of the motifs or narrative from start to finish, although of course there are developments and inconsistencies, perhaps showing different hands and the growing confidence of different embroiderers.

The history of the Tapestry[9]

Most scholars nowadays accept that the Tapestry was made in the south of England before 1082. Its purpose is unknown, but certain speculations are discussed below. It is apparently first mentioned in the fifteenth century, perhaps as early as 1463 when the accounts of Bayeux Cathedral mention repairs to a tapestry, but certainly in 1476 when it is listed in the inventory of the Cathedral of Notre-Dame of Bayeux: 'a very long and narrow hanging on which are embroidered figures and inscriptions comprising a representation of the Conquest of England, which is hung round the nave of the church on the day of the Relics and throughout the octave'.[10] Presumably because it was rolled up and stored away for most of the year the Tapestry survived fires and wars for nearly five hundred years, including two major catastrophes in the twelfth century. It was to survive unharmed but without further mention until 1724 when an accurate coloured drawing of the portion up to pl. 12 of the present book was communicated to the Académie Royale des Inscriptions et Belles-Lettres. The drawing belonged to N.J. Foucault, Intendant of Normandy (it is now in the Cabinet des Estampes of the Bibliothèque Nationale, Fol. Ad. 102), and was used by Bernard de Montfaucon as the basis for the engraving of the early scenes of the Tapestry published in the first volume of his great *Monuments de la monarchie française*, which appeared in 1729. But at that time no savant knew where the Tapestry was and indeed de Montfaucon could not have believed the accuracy of the drawing, for in engraving it he converted it to fit the forms and taste of the early eighteenth century. Eventually de Montfaucon discovered its location and sent Antoine Benoît to Bayeux to make an accurate representation of the rest of the Tapestry which was published in the second volume of the same work in 1730. Benoît's engraving served for many years as the standard source. Before de Montfaucon the Tapestry had become known, for no apparent reason, as the Tapestry of Queen Matilda (an identification still frequently met with today). The Matilda in question is identified either as the Empress Matilda, the daughter of Henry I, or more often as Matilda, the wife of William the Conqueror.

During the French Revolution the Tapestry had many adventures: on one occasion it was taken from the Cathedral to be used as a wagon cover; it was saved in dramatic fashion by a lawyer, Lambert Léonard-Leforestier. Later it was nearly cut up to make a float (of the goddess of Reason) for a carnival. It survived, however, and in 1803 was transferred to Paris at the request of Napoleon, where it was exhibited in the Museum which bore his name. This exhibition was mounted as propaganda in relation to the preparations for the invasion of England, and as such was an enormous success, politically and artistically, but with the striking of Napoleon's Boulogne camp and the abandonment of the invasion plans the Tapestry was returned to Bayeux. By 1812 it was in the Préfecture where it was wound for ease of access on two cylinders, a machine which Hudson Gurney describes as, 'like that which lets down the buckets to a well'.[11] The machine clearly damaged the Tapestry and this was commented on in 1819 by Charles Stothard,[12] who made the extremely accurate (if slightly mechanical) drawing of the embroidery for the Society of Antiquaries[13] over a period of two years. This drawing provided the basis for the first coloured reproduction of the Tapestry, in hand-tinted copper-plate engraving; it also accurately recorded the damage existing at that time. Stothard made a careful reconstruction of the missing parts by examination of the needle holes and surviving fragments of coloured thread. Very occasionally he made a mistake in his reproduction, but when this happened it was usually only a minor detail in the border. At some stage after Stothard had completed his engraving the missing parts which he had indicated were reconstructed using wools of slightly different tones from the originals.

In the 1830s a Dr Bruce saw the Tapestry and recorded that it was exhibited in eight lengths (presumably folded).[14] About 1842 the Tapestry was relined and removed to the public library of Bayeux where it was exhibited behind glass in a separate room.[15] The linen used in this relining is probably the one which survives today and which bears large hand-painted numbers identifying the individual scenes. The Tapestry was evacuated in 1870 at the time of the Franco-Prussian War but was returned to its case and remained there until 1913, when it was re-housed in the old Bishop's Palace. In 1871 it was thoroughly studied and photographed by E. Dossetter under the direction of J. Cundall for the English Board of Education and the Victoria and Albert Museum, and Dossetter's magnificent photographs were reproduced in 1873 in what is still in many respects the standard publication of the Tapestry.[16]

At the outbreak of the Second World War the Tapestry was taken down and placed in a secure vault and, after a number of alarms and excursions, moved to a safe deposit in the country at Sourches. It was then transferred to the Abbey of Juaye-Mondaye where it was studied and recorded by a German team of art-historians under the supervision of Count Metternich. Having been returned to Sourches, it remained there until 1944 when, at the time of the Allied landings in Normandy, it was sent to Paris and deposited in the cellars of the Louvre. Although there was some attempt by the Germans to remove it during the last days of the German occupation of Paris, it remained in the cellars of the Louvre until placed on exhibition in the Salle des Primitifs for just over a month in November 1944. In the following year it was returned to Bayeux and replaced on exhibition in new cases in June 1948.

More recently – in the winter of 1982/3 – the Tapestry has been cleaned and recorded under the supervision of the Sous-Direction des Monuments Historiques of the French Ministry of Culture and placed on exhibition in a new, purpose-built, museum in the shell of a converted seminary.

The historical background

The Tapestry relates, through the minds and eyes of contemporaries, the events leading up to the Norman invasion of England and culminates in a major depiction of the Battle of Hastings. Events in both England and Normandy are recounted, save for an occasional apparent solecism, in chronological order. Most scenes are easily explicable in relation to the contemporary written sources, and those which are not (particularly the much discussed Ælfgyva scene – pl. 17) are mere caesuras in a running story. The Tapestry must be seen against the background of contemporary accounts of the events which took place in the years between 1064, when Harold set out for Normandy, and Saturday, 14 October 1066, when Harold was killed by a Norman arrow at Hastings.

To understand the events portrayed in the Tapestry it is essential to try to disentangle the historical background and sort out the personalities, status and influence of the principal actors in the events of those years. First some simple genealogy. The king of England who appears in the first scene of the Tapestry is Edward, eldest son of Æthelred 'the Unready' and his formidable queen, Emma, daughter of Duke Richard I of Normandy (she was later married by Knut of Denmark, her husband's conqueror). Edward, later known as 'the Confessor', was born about 1005 and had come to the throne in 1042; he was childless.

Harold, who was to succeed him, was the son of Godwin, Earl of Wessex (died 1053), and Gytha. Gytha's sister-in-law Estrith was the daughter of Sven Forkbeard, the father of Knut the Great. Harold's sister was married to Edward the Confessor. At the time of the Conquest he was about forty-three years old and had at least two surviving brothers who appear in the Tapestry: Leofwine, the youngest, and Gyrth; both were killed at Hastings. Another brother, Tostig, Earl of Northumbria, went into exile in 1065 and was killed at Stamford Bridge. To modern eyes the most legitimate claimant to the English

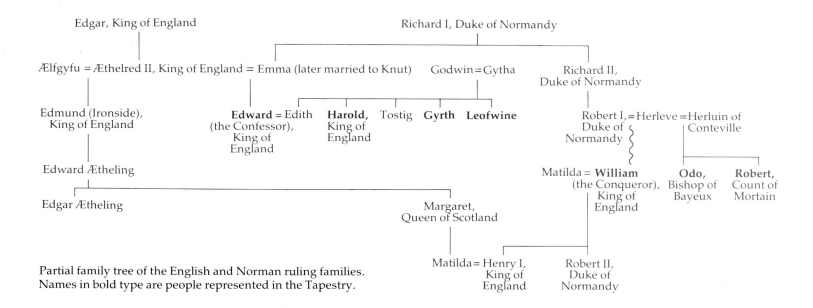

Partial family tree of the English and Norman ruling families.
Names in bold type are people represented in the Tapestry.

throne was the Ætheling (or prince) Edgar, the grandson of King Edmund Ironside and great-grandson of Æthelred, but he was too young in 1066 to take over the crown (his sister Margaret, incidentally, subsequently became Queen of Scotland and mother of Matilda, wife of Henry I).

William of Normandy (otherwise known as 'the Conqueror' or 'the Bastard') was the son and successor of Robert I, Duke of Normandy, who had died in 1035. His grandfather was the brother of Emma, Edward the Confessor's mother. He was married to Matilda of Flanders and had two half-brothers, Odo, Bishop of Bayeux, and Robert, Count of Mortain, both of whom appear in the Tapestry.

These complicated genealogies hide an even more complex family nexus (particularly in England) which had created feuds and factions for a generation. Primogeniture was not necessarily the normal means of succession: the first-born had a strong claim, but if he was too weak or (as was the case with Edgar) too young, a strong man of royal stock could be elected to the throne. Moreover, a king could in some sense nominate his heir. The important process was to be crowned; once this sacred ceremony had taken place it was difficult to challenge the anointed of God.

Of all these people Edward is perhaps the most difficult to understand. Frank Barlow has dealt with his reputation in a most succinct – if rather anti-Norman – fashion:

If Edward had been succeeded by a son, or if his actual successor, Harold, had won the battle of Hastings, it is doubtful whether later generations would have paid much attention to his reign or person, even more unlikely that he would have obtained any place at all in popular history and tradition. Edward, as we know him, is a creation of the Norman Conquest. In fact the Conquest led to the creation of two Edwards – the saint in the ecclesiastical legend and the friend of Normandy in the political legend. These two legends are not basically connected. By simplifying, we can say that the legend of Edward's holiness and justice derived at least its popular support from native English feeling – it was the work of the conquered – whereas the political legend was purely a creation of the conquerors. But it is doubtful whether the ecclesiastical legend would have

15

flourished without the support it was able to derive from the political legend. Normans could accept Edward's sanctity more easily because they believed that he had been a friend to their cause, a kinsman and benefactor.[17]

Edward was not a particularly saintly, strong or popular king, although in Barlow's words he had 'intelligence and resourcefulness, not good judgment and wisdom'. He did, however, manage to keep his kingdom unified despite the difficulties, both national and international, of the times. He had been exiled as a child to Normandy, but had returned in 1041 (when he was in his late thirties and Duke William was thirteen). He favoured Normans and was indeed a close friend of Robert, Abbot of Jumièges, who became bishop of London in 1044 and archbishop of Canterbury in 1051. Although there were many Normans at his court, he also patronized men of many other countries. Despite the events of 1051-2 – when Godwin (Harold's father) and other members of his family were outlawed, when the Queen was repudiated and when William probably visited England – it cannot be shown either that Edward at any time wanted William to succeed him or that he did not, although he seems to have dangled the succession before him. But he also seems to have dangled it before the members of the old royal line, Edward Ætheling and Edgar, and possibly before Sven Estridsson of Denmark and Harold of Wessex. William of Normandy and Harald-the-Hard-ruler (Haraldr Harðràði) of Norway had legitimate dynastic claims, and were old enough to pursue them. But Harold of Wessex, the king's brother-in-law, also had claims and is said to have been named as Edward's successor by the dying king. Edward was a powerful king and ruled over a rich, prosperous, peaceful and unified realm. He passed his kingdom entire to Harold. Harold squandered the inheritance. The Norman sources unanimously say, however, that William was the true heir and that Harold was his dependant.

Harold has had a mixed reception from the historians and chroniclers.[18] He was seen by the Normans as a vicious oath-breaker, usurper and all-round villain. His claim to royal blood was thin. Even the English were not so sure that his claims were legitimate; after his death they turned their attention not to his kin but to members of the old English line – Edgar, Margaret of Scotland, Waltheof – as claimants. And yet in the Tapestry Harold is described as *Rex*, he is portrayed in heroic style and dies a hero's death. In the *Vita Ædwardi* he is eulogized, 'a true friend of his race and country, who guided his father's powers even more actively, and walked in his ways, that is in patience and mercy with kindness to men of goodwill. But disturbers of the peace, thieves and robbers, this champion of the law threatened with the terrible face of a lion',[19] which is laying it on a bit! Harold was a tough and experienced soldier and with his brothers held enormous political and landed power in England, controlling vast tracts of the country from Northumbria to the south coast; Harold himself also became a brutal and very successful hammer of the Welsh and (as seen in the Tapestry) a companion in arms of William during the latter's assault on Brittany. The title *dux Anglorum* given to Harold in the first scenes of the Tapestry testifies to his supreme position in the country at the start of the adventures depicted there.

The third character in the story can best be described as shrewd. William, Duke of Normandy,[20] was, like Harold, tough, brash and violent, but was endowed with a strength of purpose and political know-how which outstripped most of his contemporaries. His marriage, to Matilda of Flanders – for which he fought long and hard against the Church – was not only a political and dynastic success: he also gained a strong-minded wife. William was the illegitimate son of Robert I, sixth Duke of Normandy, by Herleve, the daughter of a tanner (she later married Herluin of Conteville and produced two sons – William's half-brothers Odo, later bishop of Bayeux, and Robert, Count of Mortain). William's father died on pilgrimage in Asia Minor in 1035 having named his son as heir. Strong hands protected the seven-year-old William – Archbishop Robert of Rouen, Alan of Brittany, Osbern the steward and Turold, the child's tutor. The times were, however, tough; near-anarchy reigned and soon his protectors were all dead and replaced by others as a blood-bath developed in Normandy. By 1046 the young William was surrounded by trouble, revolt sprang up on every hand (but particularly in the west of the duchy) with the avowed object of overthrowing him. Supported by Henry of France, William defeated the rebellious Norman *vicomtes* at Val-ès-Dunes and the tide turned. But all was not over; for thirteen years William continued to fight on all sides, against his own magnates, against the French king and against many permutations of French and Norman leaders. William, through great qualities of leadership, by cunning and by increasing vigilance, managed to survive these years and emerge in 1060, with the deaths of Geoffrey of Anjou and Henry of France, as the formidable, strong and powerful ruler who appears in the early scenes of the Tapestry.

These three men dominate the Tapestry and rightly so, for it was their enterprise, their political decisions and their military actions which conditioned the story told there. The other personalities represented on the hanging – Harold's brothers, William's brothers, the counts, lords and other characters – may have been (or at least some of them may have been) important, but they are comparatively minor actors on the stage. Their rôle adds tension to the story, but is not paramount. The drama is played out between Harold and William.

The Tapestry as an historical source

History is not a series of vignettes, it is a continuing process, one moment running into the next, with continuous reference back – interpreted with hindsight. It would therefore be too much to hope that the Bayeux Tapestry, which presents us with a series of vignettes, would provide a coherent consecutive account of events. It is, however, much more than the strip cartoon to which it has often been compared; it is rather a subtle chronicle of the events it portrays. There is no need for the word 'Wham!' to be written above a scene of brutal death; there is no call for a ballooned phrase starting with the word 'Thinks: . . .'. Its audience was sophisticated or knowledgeable enough to understand its subtleties, and sophisticated enough to be able to put a gloss on its obscurities. There was no need, for instance, for the Tapestry designer to explain the enigmatic scene (pl. 17) which is labelled, 'where a certain cleric and Ælfgyva'. The story was presumably notorious, clear in the memory of the audience, easily explainable and possibly rather distasteful. That it reflects a scandal seems reasonably certain – a sordid affair can often shake great men or affect history. This scandal must have been significant in relation to the story told by the Tapestry, but it is here inserted with economy and tact and is perhaps referred to in the lower border by means of a scene of overtly sexual character.

Fortunately such puzzling scenes are rare in the Tapestry; most are capable of interpretation in the light of other historical sources. Sometimes the Tapestry reverses scenes chronologically – for example, Edward's burial is portrayed before his death. Occasionally a figure will appear with what seems undue prominence – Turold (pl. 11), for example – but generally the story is clear and consecutive, although by its nature episodic. Even the final battle scene with all its movement and tension is no more than a vignette. This is not to condemn the Tapestry as an historical source; it is the most vivid surviving record of this particular phase of English history, standing alongside the weighed or weighted words of the chronicler or historian.[21] According to David Douglas, perhaps the greatest historian of this period, 'it may be accepted, therefore, without much misgiving, that the main body of the Bayeux Tapestry constitutes a primary source for the history of England in this age, and one which in this respect deserves to be studied alongside the accounts in the Anglo-Saxon Chronicle and in William of Poitiers'.[22]

What, then, are the other contemporary sources and what value have they? The Anglo-Saxon Chronicle, as we have seen,[23] is laconic, short and pious. It is a primary but largely uninformative source concerning the events depicted in the Tapestry. There is nothing in the Chronicle which refers to any scene in the Tapestry other than the consecration of Westminster Abbey, the death of Edward, the accession of Harold, the appearance of Halley's comet and the Battle of Hastings. Henry Loyn does, however, suggest that the designer of the Tapestry relied on a version of the Chronicle,[24] but of this there is no hard evidence.

William of Jumièges, a Norman monk, provides us with a short but good source for the events of the period; he also provides a parallel to the story as told in the Bayeux Tapestry. His account forms part of the seventh book of *Gesta Normannorum Ducum*[25] (The Deeds of the Duke of the Normans . . .). It is generally accepted that it was written in or shortly after 1070. The story he tells is summary, but while he does not deny the Tapestry at any point, certain actions (the imprisonment of Harold by Guy of Ponthieu, for example) and the interpretation put on some of the events are not exactly the same. He can also make mistakes – he says, for instance, that Harold fell at the beginning rather than at the end of the Battle of Hastings.

William of Poitiers provides by far the most detailed account of the events covered by the Tapestry. William was Archdeacon of Lisieux and one of the king's chaplains. Very much in the centre of events, he appears to have written the *Gesta Willelmi ducis Normannorum et regis Anglorum*[26] (The Deeds of William, Duke of the Normans and King of the English) between 1071 and 1077. Recent scholars, Drögereit[27] and Loyn[28] for example, have suggested that the designer of the Tapestry actually knew William of Poitiers' account. Brooks and Walker, however, have argued convincingly that this is unlikely, postulating that both sources reflect the version of the events of the critical years that was current and acceptable to the Normans of the 1070s.[29] William of Poitiers gives a view of the events leading up to the Conquest which states the Norman case, 'to show that the conquest of England was just and inevitable';[30] his account is particularly valuable in relation to the Battle of Hastings.

An enigmatic and much discussed source is the *Vita Ædwardi Regis* (The Life of King Edward the Confessor), written by a foreigner living in England (possibly a monk of St Bertin, St-Omer), who had sources at the royal court and in Flanders. The Life was written in two parts. The dating is complicated but there is general, although not universal, agreement that the first part of the Life was written before Hastings, the second before 1070. The book is largely hagiography, but, if used with great care, is a useful quarry for certain historical sidelights on events which took place before the king's death.[31]

Other texts can be used to illuminate the period, but used with caution because they were written down so much later. Chief among these are the annals ascribed to Florence of Worcester,[32] which (although compiled in the first quarter of the twelfth century) enshrine in a fairly plodding fashion the events of the period, perhaps based in part on a lost version of the Anglo-Saxon Chronicle. This, like other later sources – William of Malmesbury and Henry of Huntingdon, for example – must be used highly critically, while the *Carmen de Hastingae Proelio* (The Song of the Battle of Hastings) has now been completely re-dated[33] and has little historical credibility.

Basically we depend on William of Poitiers and the Bayeux Tapestry for our knowledge of most of the events of 1066; other sources help us but must be used with care. Without the Tapestry, then, our knowledge of the history of the Norman Conquest and the events which led up to it would be much poorer and more episodic. It is, as David Douglas wrote, 'a primary source' for the period.

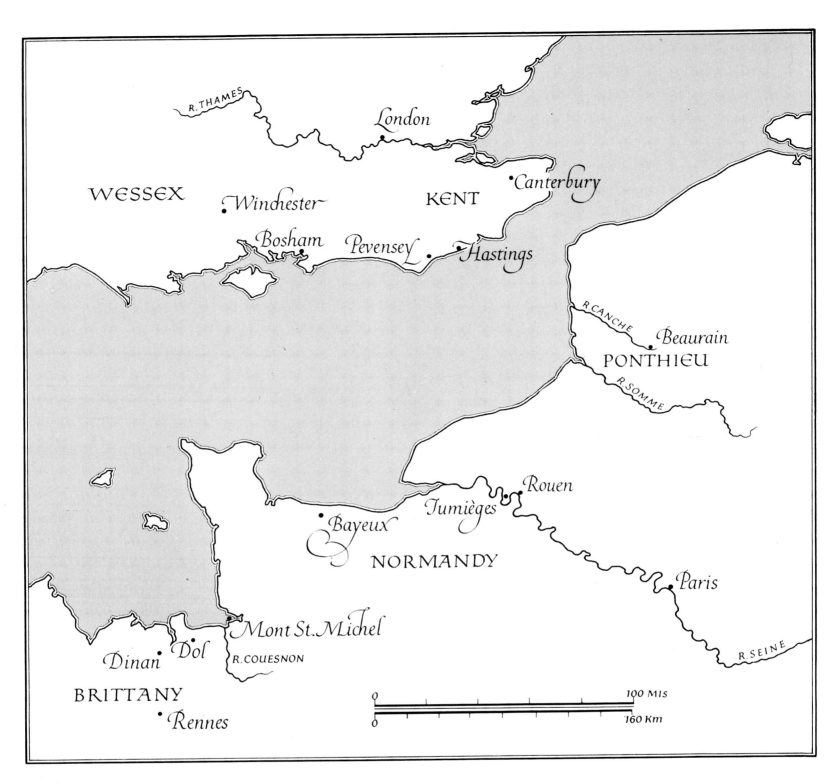

Map of south-east England and north-west France in 1066, showing the places mentioned in the text.

THE PLATES

For a detailed commentary see
pp. 174–95. For a translation of the
Latin inscriptions see pp. 172–3.
Opposite: detail of pl. 24: William gives
arms to Harold. Reproduced actual size.

1 King Edward the Confessor addresses
Harold, who departs (right) on
horseback.

2 Harold and his knights ride with hawk
and hounds to Bosham.

3 The church and (on the right) Harold's
manor of Bosham, with men feasting in
an upper room.

4 Harold and his men take ship for
Normandy.

5 Harold's ship on the way to Normandy.

6 Harold's ship reaches Normandy, and
he disembarks.

7 Guy, Count of Ponthieu, takes Harold
prisoner. Right: Guy and his soldiers.

8 Guy and his retinue ride with Harold to
the castle of Beaurain.

9 Harold arrives at Beaurain and is
addressed by Guy.

10 Left: Guy speaking to Harold. Right:
Guy listens to a messenger sent from
Duke William.

11 William's messengers arrive at Guy's
castle; a groom holds the horses.

12 William's messengers on their way.
Right: men bringing the news about
Harold to Duke William.

13 Left: William listens to the messengers.
Centre: William's castle. Right: part of
Guy's retinue taking Harold to William.

14 Guy and Harold ride to meet William
(right).

15 Left: William and his men meet Guy and
Harold. Right: they set off for William's
palace.

16 The party arrives at William's palace.
Right: William, inside the palace, gives
audience.

17 Left: William talks to Harold. Right:
Ælfgyva and a cleric – an unexplained
episode.

18 William and his army, with Harold, set
off on an expedition against Conan of
Brittany.

19 With Mont St Michel in the background,
the troops try to cross the river
Couesnon but some sink into the
quicksands.

20 Left: Harold rescues two men from the
sands. Right: the army attacks Conan,
who flees from Dol.

21 Left: the town of Dol. Right: Conan's
men in flight.

22 Left: the town of Rennes. Right:
William's army attacks Dinan, where
Conan has taken refuge.

23 The attack on Dinan. Right: Conan
surrenders the keys.

24 Left: William's soldiers receiving the
keys. Centre: William gives arms to
Harold. Right: William and Harold set
off for Bayeux.

25 They arrive at Bayeux. Right: William
presides at the oath-taking ceremony.

26 Left: Harold swearing an oath to William
between two reliquaries. Right: he sets
sail for England.

27 Harold lands and sets off to present
himself to King Edward.

28 Harold is received by King Edward.

29 King Edward's body is borne to
Westminster Abbey.

30 Right: King Edward on his deathbed,
and (below) his body is laid out. Left:
part of the funeral procession.

31 Left: Harold is given the crown. Right:
he sits enthroned as king.

32 Left: attendants at the enthronement.
Centre: men wonder at an unusual 'star'
(Halley's comet). Right: a man brings
news to Harold.

33 An English ship, bearing news of
Harold's accession, sets out for
Normandy.

34 Left: the ship arrives in Normandy.
Right: William in his palace.

35 William orders his men to build ships,
and (right) they begin cutting down
trees.

36 Shipbuilding.

37 The ships are taken to the sea.

38 Armour, weapons and supplies are
carried to the ships.

39 William and his army prepare to embark.

40,41,42 The Norman army at sea.

43 The Normans arrive at Pevensey; horses
are disembarked.

44 The ships are drawn up on the shore and
troops set off for Hastings.

45 Mounted soldiers forage for food from
the English.

46 Wadard and, right, the preparation of
the feast.

47 Meat is cooked and passed to an
extempore sideboard made of shields.

48 Left: Bishop Odo blesses the food and
drink. Right: William, flanked by his
half-brothers Bishop Odo and Robert of
Mortain.

49 Norman workmen with spades build a
fortification; two of them (centre) are
quarrelling.

50 Centre: a messenger brings news to
William of the approach of Harold's
army. Right: a house is set on fire and a
woman and a boy escape.

51 William, leaving Hastings, prepares to
mount.

52 The Norman knights set off for the
battlefield.

53 Norman knights on their way to the
battlefield.

54 William at the head of his troops meets
Vital.

55 Left: Vital gives William information
about the English army. Right: two
Norman knights.

56 English scouts observe William's
approach and bring news to Harold.

57 William exhorts his troops before the
battle.

58 The Norman knights begin their attack.

59 Norman knights riding against the
English.

60 Norman knights, supported by archers
on foot, attack the English.

61 Norman knights clash with the English,
who fight on foot. (From this point the
border is filled with dead and mutilated
bodies.)

62 English foot-soldiers attacked by
mounted Normans.

63 Norman knights on the attack.

64 Harold's two brothers are killed.

65 Hand-to-hand fighting between
Normans and English.

66 Norman knights attack the English on a
hill.

67 Bishop Odo, holding a wand, rallies his
men.

68 Norman knights; William raises his
helmet in order to be recognized. (In the
border are bowmen.)

69 Norman knights attack English infantry.

70 English soldiers surrounding Harold are
killed.

71 Harold is killed. (In the border, bodies
being stripped of their armour.)

72 The English fall and flee.

73 The English in flight.

THE TAPESTRY

Fold out ▷

WILLELM: hAROLD

1

REX: UBI: HAROLD DV

O DVX · ANGLORVM : ET SVI N

OS hAM: ECCLESIA

3

HIC HAROLD MA

4

RE NAVIGAVIT ET VE

…LIS:VENTO:PLENIS
=NIT:INTE RR A:
VVIDONIS
COMITIS

5

6

HAROLD: hIC:A

ET I BI EVM:TEN VIT :

UBI·HAROLD : 7WIDO

UBI:HAROLD:DUX:ANGLORUM:ET:SUI:MILITES:EQUITANT:AD:BOSHAM:

VIDO:PARABO LANT:

10

UBI:NUNTII:WIL

VILLELMI : DVCIS : VENE

TVROLD

11

...VNT:ADVVIDO
NE

NVNTII : WIL

…I: NVNTIVS:ADWIL GELMVM DVCEM

13

HIC : WIDO : AD

DUXIT HAROLDUM ADVV

M : DVCEM

HIC·DVX·

: VVILGELM : CVM hAROLDO

16

17

UBI:UNUS:CLERICUS:ET: · hIC

ÆLFGY VA

WILLEM:DVX:ET EXERCIT

18

...VS:EIVS:VENERVNT:ADMON...

TE MICHAELIS E

19

THIC : TRANSIERVNT : FLVM

hIC : HAROLD : D

DEAREI

MEN : COSNONIS : ET VENER
DVX : TRAhEBAT : EOS

ENA

NT AD DOL : ET : CONA

ONAN :   FVGA VER

HIC MILITES ... WILL ...

... NES ...

…LMI:DVCIS:PVG…NANT:C…

:CONTRA

23

DINA NTES : ET : CVNAN : C L

...AVES:POR REXIT : hIC:WIL...
DEDIT : ...
ARMA

...ELM:
...A ROL DO:
hIE
WIL...

...ELM VENIT : BAGIAS

UBI hAROLD ⫶ SACRAMEN
VVILLELMO D

ENTVM:FECIT:⋄ HIC HAROL
D DVCI:⁒

O: DVX:

REVERSVS : EST

AD ANGLICAM:TERRAM:

M :· ET VENIT : AD : EDVVA

28

M: HIC PORTATVR: CORP

29

VS:EADWARDI:REGIS:AD:E

D:ECCLESIAM:SCI
PETRI APLI

ETHI

HIC EADWARDVS:REX

ILECTO:ALLOQVITEIDELES:

HIC

DEFVNCTVS

EST

.DEDERVNT:HAROLDO:

:ORO ÑA: REGIS

IC RE SIDET:HAROLD
EX:AN GLORVM:
STIGANT
ARCHIEPS

ISTI MIRAN

ᚺIC:M

…AVIS:ANGLI

CA·VENIT·INTER
WILLELMI·DV

HIC TRAHVNT:NAVES:A

DMA RE:·

ISTI

...ES: ETHIC +HIC: WILL...
...NT: CARRVM
...NO: ETARMIS :·

ELM: DVX INMAGN O:N

...NAVIGIO:

40

MAR E

TRAN

41

...SIVIT...ETV...

...VENIT AD PEVENESÆ:·:

HIC EXE

...VIBVS ·— ETHIC:MILITES:

ESTINA ... VERV ... NT:hES

ESTINGA : UT CIBUM . RA

45

ERENTVR:

HIC:EST:VVAD AR D:

HIC:COQVI
TVR:CARO

ETHI

47

HIC FECERVN : PRANDIVM :

48

ODO·EPS· ROTBERT·

WILLELM·

ISTE·IVSSIT:VT·EODE·RETVR

49

CASTELLVM·AT·HESTENGA·CEA

…EASTRA   HIC:NVNTIA… WILLELM…

50

…TUM EST: hIC DOM…
…FHAROLD: CEN…

DOMVS:IN
CENDITVR:

51

HIC:MILITES:EXIERVNT:DE

ƐHƐSƬƐИGA :

ET:VENERVNT

AD P

53

...RELIVM: CON TRA. HAROL D...

...DVM·REGE: HIC: VVILLE[...]

54

M:DVX INTERROGAT:VIT

VITAL: SI VI DISSET

HAROLDI

EXERCI
TV

ISTE

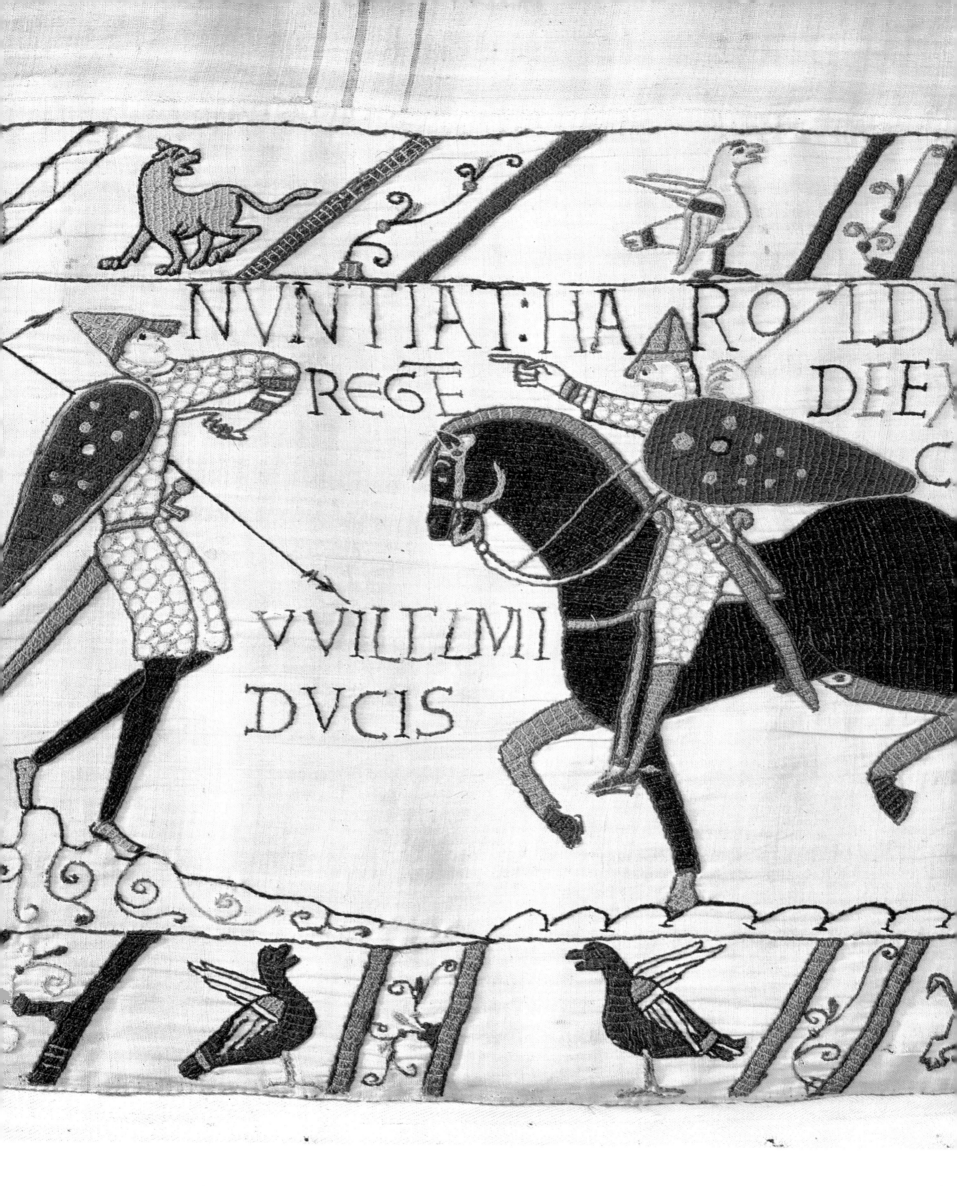

NVNTIAT HAROLDV

REGE

DEEX

VVILELMI

DVCIS

:DVX ⊢ ALLOQVITVR·SV

IS·MILITI BVS·VT·PREPARA

...ARENSE: VI RILI TER

ET SAP

CON RA

60

XERCITV·

HIC CECI

...DERVNT ALEVV...

VUINE · ET : GVRÐ

64

FRATRES:HAROLDI

...REGIS: HIC CC...

HIC·ODO·E

67

S: BACVLV· TENENS· CONF

ETCECI DE

RVNT Q

IERANT·CVM·HAROLDO ·:·

HIC

ET FVGA:VE RTER

58

ANGLI

73

Tailpiece: details from the border, pls. 16
(top), 14–15 (centre) and 17 (bottom).

I   The Inscriptions

THIS is a simplified plain text and translation of the inscriptions on the Tapestry. The inscription as seen on the Tapestry is restored in one or two places, but is largely complete. Only occasionally is there anything more than a minor doubt concerning a reading, as in the orthography of the king's name in pl. 1. The text is worked in black or dark green wool for the first half of the Tapestry, but from pl. 48 letters are executed in sage green and terracotta alternately.

A transliteration and discussion of the epigraphy was published by Wormald.[34] I have followed his normalization in my transcription, but have ignored the symbols used for word division, of which there are six main forms. I have, however, punctuated *ad lib.* in the translation and capitalized proper names in the Latin text. Letters underlined represent contractions in the original. I have tried in my translation, like Wormald, to do battle with the rapid changes of tense, but I may not always have achieved total consistency.

Plate 1	*Edward rex*[35]	King Edward.	
1–2	*Ubi Harold dux Anglorum et sui milites equitant ad Bosham*	Where Harold, an earl[36] of the English, and his soldiers ride to Bosham.	
3	*Æcclesia*	The church.	
4	*Hic Harold mare navigavit*	Here Harold sailed the sea	
4–5	*et velis vento plenis venit in terram Widonis comitis*	and, the wind full in his sails, he came to the country of Count Guy.	
6	*Harold*	Harold.	
6–7	*Hic apprehendit Wido Haroldum*	Here Guy arrests Harold	
7–8	*et duxit eum ad Belrem et ibi eum tenuit*	and led him to Beaurain and kept him there.	
9–10	*Ubi Harold et Wido parabolant*	Where Harold and Guy talk.	
10–11	*Ubi nuntii Willelmi ducis venerunt ad Widonem*	Where the messengers of Duke William came to Guy.	
11	*Turold*[37]	Turold	
12	*Nuntii Willelmi*	The messengers of William.	
12–13	*Hic venit nuntius ad Wilgelmum ducem*	Here came a messenger to Duke William.	
13–15	*Hic Wido adduxit Haroldum ad Wilgelmum Normannorum ducem*	Here Guy brought Harold to William Duke of the Normans.	
15–16	*Hic dux Wilgelm cum Haroldo venit ad palatium suum*	Here Duke William came with Harold to his palace.	
17	*Ubi unus clericus et Ælfgyva*	Where a certain cleric and Ælfgyva.	
17–19	*Hic Willem dux et exercitus eius venerunt ad montem Michaelis*	Here Duke William and his army came to Mont St Michel	

19–20	*et hic transierunt flumen Cosnonis. Hic Harold dux trahebat eos de arena*	and here they crossed the river Couesnon. Here Duke Harold pulled them out of the sand	
20–21	*et venerunt ad Dol et Conan fuga vertit*	and they came to Dol and Conan turned to flight.	
21–22	*Rednes*	Rennes.	
22–23	*Hic milites Willelmi ducis pugnant contra Dinantes*	Here Duke William's soldiers fight against the men of Dinan	
23–24	*et Cunan claves porrexit*	and Conan surrendered the keys.	
24	*Hic Willelm dedit Haroldo arma*	Here William gave arms to Harold.	
24–25	*Hic Willelm venit Bagias*	Here William came to Bayeux.	
25–26	*Ubi Harold sacramentum fecit Willelmo duci*	Where Harold made an oath to Duke William.	
26–27	*Hic Harold dux reversus est ad Anglicam terram*	Here Duke Harold returned to the English country	
28	*et venit ad Edwardum regem*	and came to King Edward.	
29–30	*Hic portatur corpus Eadwardi regis ad ecclesiam sancti Petri Apostoli*	Here the body of King Edward is carried to the church of St Peter the Apostle.	
30	*Hic Eadwardus rex in lecto alloquitur fideles*	Here King Edward in bed talks to his faithful followers	
30	*et hic defunctus est*	and here he is dead.	
31	*Hic dederunt Haroldo coronam regis*	Here they have given the crown of the king to Harold.	
31	*Hic residet Harold rex Anglorum*	Here sits throned Harold, King of the English.	

31	*Stigant archiepiscopus*	Stigand, archbishop.
32	*Isti mirant(ur)[38] stellam*	These men marvel at the star.
32	*Harold*	Harold.
33–34	*Hic navis Anglica venit in terram Willelmi ducis*	Here an English ship came to the country of Duke William.
34–35	*Hic Willelm dux iussit naves edificare*	Here Duke William ordered ships to be built.
37	*Hic trahuntur naves ad mare*	Here ships are hauled to the sea.
38–39	*Isti portant armas ad naves, et hic trahunt carrum cum vino et armis*	These men carry arms to the ships, and here they pull a wagon with wine and arms.
39–42	*+ Hic Willelm dux in magno navigio mare transivit et venit ad Pevenesæ*	Here Duke William in a great ship crossed the sea and came to Pevensey.
43–44	*Hic exeunt caballi de navibus*	Here the horses leave the boats
44–45	*et hic milites festinaverunt Hestinga ut cibum raperentur*	and here soldiers have hurried to Hastings to seize food.
46	*Hic est Wadard*	Here is Wadard.
46	*Hic coquitur caro*	Here the meat is cooked,
46–47	*et hic ministraverunt*	and here it has been served.
47	*Ministri[39]*	The servants.
47	*Hic fecerunt prandium*	Here they made a meal,
48	*et hic episcopus cibum et potum benedicit*	and here the bishop blesses the food and drink.
48	*Odo episcopus Willelm Rotbert*	Bishop Odo, William, Robert.
49	*Iste iussit ut foderetur castellum at Hestengaceastra[40]*	This man has commanded that a fortification should be thrown up at Hastings.
50	*Hic nuntiatum est Willelmo de Harold(o)*	Here news is brought to William about Harold.
50–51	*Hic domus incenditur*	Here a house is burned.
51–54	*Hic milites exierunt de Hestenga et venerunt ad prelium contra Haroldum rege(m)*	Here the soldiers went out of Hastings and came to the battle against King Harold.
54–55	*Hic Willelm dux interrogat Vital si vidisset exercitum Haroldi*	Here Duke William asks Vital whether he has seen Harold's army.
56	*Iste nuntiat Haroldum regem de exercitu Wilelmi ducis*	This man tells King Harold about Duke William's army.
57–61	*Hic Willelm dux alloquitur suis militibus ut prepararent se viriliter et sapienter ad prelium contra Anglorum exercitum*	Here Duke William exhorts his soldiers that they prepare themselves manfully and wisely for the battle against the army of the English.
63–64	*Hic ceciderunt Lewine et Gyrth fratres Haroldi regis*	Here were killed Leofwine and Gyrth, the brothers of King Harold.
65–66	*Hic ceciderunt simul Angli et Franci in prelio*	Here at the same time English and French fell in battle.
67	*Hic Odo episcopus baculum tenens confortat pueros*	Here Bishop Odo holding a wand encourages the young men.
68	*Hic est dux Wilelmus*	Here is Duke William.
68	*E(usta)tius[41]*	Eustace.
68–70	*Hic Franci pugnant et ceciderunt qui erant cum Haroldo*	Here the French fight and have killed those who were with Harold.
71	*Hic Harold rex interfectus est*	Here King Harold has been killed
72–73	*et fuga verterunt Angli*	and the English have turned to flight.

1

II The Commentary

1–3 It is early 1064,[42] and King Edward, crowned and sceptred, enthroned in state (as on his seal)[43] in the hall of his palace probably in Winchester, gives instruction to Earl Harold.

Harold rides to his manor at Bosham with his hawk and hunting dogs followed by a group of his retainers (note '*sui* milites'). Harold and a retainer approach in a position of humility the church at Bosham.

The facade of the palace in pl. 1 is flanked by corner towers with a central doorway and a diapered wall. There is a hint of drapery in the roof above the king's head. The vegetal ornament, top left in the border, perhaps reflects an English phase of the Scandinavian Ringerike style.

The portion of the Tapestry in pl. 1 is much damaged and the linen is much repaired; some of the tendrils in the left-hand border are rather clumsily over-restored and part of the panelling on the facade of the hall is apparently restored.[44] The first four letters of the name EDWARD do not appear in the earliest reproduction of the Tapestry, nor does most of the V of VBI. The middle letters of Harold's name have also been restored.[45]

The dogs (pls. 2-3) are coursing two 'hares' and

4   5

3–6 Harold feasts on the upper floor of what is presumably his manor at Bosham. His men (one standing on an external staircase) tell Harold that his ship is ready and, carrying his hawk in his hand and with tunic tucked up to his waist, he embarks accompanied by men carrying dogs and sweeps and poles. The mast and anchor are raised and the oarsmen start to row whilst another man poles off. The wind fills the sails and the ship or ships cross the Channel, to cast anchor and unstep the mast on the shores of Ponthieu.

William of Malmesbury tells that Harold sailed from Bosham,[46] but this late source may itself be based on the Tapestry. Bosham controlled Chichester haven and was perhaps the most important and richest estate in Sussex, held originally by Harold's father, Godwin; it was held by the king and Bishop Osbern of Exeter at the time of Domesday.[47]

The feast may be compared with the more richly furnished – if alfresco – meal in pl. 48. The men drink from horns and bowls; the man at the top of the stairs has a knife. The only surviving horn of anything like this date comes from Holland and is much restored

have leash-rings or bells pendant from their collars (in pl. 4 this feature does not appear; I therefore suspect that bells are represented). The hawk has jesses but no hood. All the men have moustaches and are dressed in cloaks and tunics. The horses' manes are hogged or tightly braided. The spurs are missing through damage on all the riders save Harold; he wears a prick-spur of a type found on practically every other rider in the Tapestry. The reins on the farthest rider in the centre are also detailed in a fashion found elsewhere in the Tapestry. Each rein ends in a strap-end and is joined above the rider's

hand by a button or circular slide. The tree forms an end to this scene. The crosses at the gables of the church at Bosham distinguish it from a secular building.

The cross element of the final T of EQUITANT, much of the D of AD and the BOS have been repaired, but the stitch marks show that the reconstruction is correct. Other repairs are obvious: it should be noted that the line which forms the upper edge of the embroidery is much repaired, as elsewhere in the Tapestry.

but must belong to the late tenth century; the animal-head terminal and large mount at the mouth have a long tradition in England.[48] One of the men carrying oars to the ship also carries a bent object of unknown use which has a remarkable iron parallel in the Viking Age ship burial from the Ile de Groix.[49] The ship's boat (pl. 5) is paralleled in the ninth-century burial from Gokstad, Norway.[50] The shields at the stern of the ships may have had some significance, while those that line the side perhaps shielded the crew from spray when under sail. Clear details are given of

the preparation of the ships for departure and landing. Note the rope in the ship to the left in pl. 6 which is paralleled in pl. 33 – is it a fishing line? The tendril, top left in pl. 6, has a clear Ringerike form.

The lower borders depict scenes from Aesop's fables: the raven, the fox and the piece of cheese; the wolf and the lamb drinking at the river; the pregnant bitch (pl.4); the crane removing a bone from the wolf's throat; the lion and his subjects (pl. 5; note the monkey represented as a naked human).[51]

7

8

7–10 Harold, coming ashore from his anchored ships, unarmed and apparently unprepared, is seized quite violently by armed soldiers of Guy, Count of Ponthieu, a small province to the north of Normandy. Guy, mounted and armed with a sword, directs the arrest. Harold and Guy, both carrying hawks and followed by dogs and armed soldiers, ride to Guy's residence at Beaurain. Leaving his followers outside the hall, Harold enters and, holding his unbelted and sheathed sword, has an interview with Guy. To the right of Guy a soldier points towards William's mes-

sengers in the next scene, while another man apparently sneaks off to tell William of Harold's arrival. The three events are telescoped into one. Both William of Jumièges and William of Poitiers[52] say that Harold was thrown into prison, but the Tapestry is probably more accurate – a captive of Harold's eminence would have been treated with great respect.

An early medieval anchor of this form is known from Ribe, Denmark.[53] The swords held by Harold and another man in pl. 9 show the method of fasten-

11

12

10–13 There seems to be a reversal of events at this point. In pl. 13 William, sitting outside what are possibly the town walls of Rouen, receives messengers telling of Harold's capture by Guy. Messengers from William ride to Guy (pl. 12) asking for the release of Harold (pls. 10-11), while a dwarf holds their horses. Guy receives them standing and holding an axe. One of the messengers, the gesticulating man in pl. 10, is often identified as the Turold whose name is inscribed above the dwarf. It is not impossible that Turold is the dwarf himself; to me the identifying label is too far away from the chief messenger to be a

convincing designation (compare, for example, Stigand in pl. 31, Wadard in pl. 46, William, Odo and Robert in pl. 48 and William in pl. 56). Turold was a common name and for this reason the identification with Turold, Constable of Bayeux, has been much questioned.[57] I feel rather attracted by the idea that Turold is the bearded dwarf and is the artist of the Tapestry.[58]

The two horses in pl. 11 give a clear view of the horse's tack. Like all saddles in the Tapestry these have a high bow and cantle, with a girth buckled at the side and attached underneath the saddle by

9   10

ing the belt: in one case with two belt slides, in the other with a strap-end and a belt slide. In pl. 8 Guy is shown in semi-majesty, enthroned and with his sword held as a sword of state.[54] At the beginning of this sequence the French do not have bare necks in the manner of the Normans depicted later in the Tapestry, but from pl. 9 onwards there is an attempt to differentiate Norman and English (the English usually being moustachioed).

The fables depicted in the lower border represent the envious fox; the cow, the sheep and the goat

hunting with the lion; and what has been identified as either the lion and the donkey[55] or the wolf and the stag.[56]

There are a number of obvious repairs. In pl. 7 the yellow wool on the anchor is a replacement, and the upper border has been replaced since Stothard's engraving between the first E of *Apprehendit* and the O of *Haroldus*. The upper border in pl. 8 has been replaced between the two Es.

13

rivets. The stirrup leathers are adjustable (the riders' legs are usually only slightly bent) and the stirrups are clearly drawn. The breast-band has a pendant at its junction with the saddle. The reins consist of two straps held together on one of the two horses by buttons or slides below the jaw and towards the man's hand. They may also have strap-ends. The wooden portion of a late medieval saddle with bow and high cantle of this form is recorded by Carol Morris from Beverley,[59] and a ninth-century saddle bow of rather different form comes from Coppergate, York.[60] The

form of the stirrup is close to that generally found in tenth- and eleventh-century England.[61]

The ploughing, harrowing and bird-scaring scene in the lower border has been identified as Aesop's fable of the swallow and the birds, whilst the scene which looks like bear-baiting has been identified as the knight and the wild boar, but this has been questioned, as has the identity of the hunting scene (pls. 12-13).[62] Ploughs occur commonly in Anglo-Saxon manuscripts,[63] but this is the only occurrence of a harrow. For the sling, see p. 210.

14   15

13–17 Guy and Harold, both holding hawks, ride to William, who meets them halfway and conducts Harold to the palace at Rouen. William's and Guy's entourages are armed and carry shields. Harold is treated with respect. The Tapestry agrees with William of Poitiers who states that Guy surrendered Harold in person, in return for a considerable ransom, and that William brought Harold to Rouen.[64]

    William's cloak is far from conventional; the pair of ribbons fluttering from his neck also appear in pl. 24.

    The palace of Duke William is an imposing and

large building. William, holding his sword, sits on a cushioned chair which is grander than those seen in pls. 10 and 13. The animal-head post at his back may well be related to similar posts found in the ship-burial from Oseberg, Norway, which may have come from a royal court and which (although of ninth-century date) are clearly related to later medieval chairs in Scandinavia.[65]

    The borders are not without interest. The mounted man, lower border left (pl. 13), may be whirling a sling, or may carry a club (cf. pl. 7). There are a pair of

18   19

17–20 An enigmatic scene treats of a woman with an English name, Ælfgyva, and 'a certain cleric'. It may represent rape or adultery; the cleric may be making a pass, or slapping the woman for having impure thoughts or for being a witch. The possibilities are endless, but the explicitly male naked figure in the border below perhaps suggests a sexual subject. An unconvincing attempt has been made to identify the lady with Queen Ælfgyfu, wife of Æthelred II,[68] but this is but the latest of a series of investigations into a scene which must have meant something to the con-

temporary audience but which, in the absence of further evidence, means nothing to us.

    Following this scene, William, accompanied by Harold, sets out on a military campaign against Duke Conan II of Brittany. Passing Mont St Michel they ride to Dol. Some soldiers get into trouble in the quicksands of the River Couesnon and two of them are rescued by Harold.

    Ælfgyva is represented within a frame reminiscent of the frames of the Winchester School of manuscripts, placed rather like Ætheldreda in the Benedic-

camels with terribly unconvincing humps in the border above William (pls. 14-15) and peacocks in the border above William's palace (pl. 17). The scene of the naked lady and the phallic gentleman in the lower border of pl. 14 has been optimistically identified as one of Aesop's fables, the virgin and the suitors,[66] but the connection is tenuous and it should perhaps be treated more simply as a scene of sexual assault. A strenuous attempt has also been made to fit the naked man with the axe (pl. 17) within the Aesop canon,[67] but this is hardly convincing; what the man

is doing with an axe in such a situation does, however, put a strain on the imagination.

To the left of the tree in pl. 15 the linen base of the Tapestry has been joined (the join can just be detected below the patch). The upper border at this point is out of register and there is a minimum of embroidery covering the join. This is the most obvious join in the Tapestry.

tional of St Æthelwold.[69] The cleric is tonsured and only his hand appears within the frame. The tower to the left presumably signifies the boundary of the palace complex at Rouen, but also acts as a punctuation mark. William is probably the figure (pls. 18–19) in the multicoloured clothes bearing a club but no other weapon. The banner in pl. 18 is attached to a lance, the weight of which is taken in the stirrup.

The lower border contains (pl. 18) another scene from the fable of the crow, the fox and the cheese. In the border below the River Couesnon are fishes and

eels, also a man with a knife in his hand who is either drowning or catching eels. The eagle and other animals, one of whose tails is held by a centaur, have been identified, perhaps with little reason, as representations of constellations.[70] In the upper margin to the right of Mont St Michel is a man seated in a chair (similar to that in pl. 16), his arm stretched out as though in benediction.

21-24 The story of the campaign in Brittany. Dol is captured; the army rides on to Rennes and Dinan is taken. Conan, having escaped by a rope from Dol, surrenders the keys of Dinan on the end of a beflagged lance to William, who receives them in like manner. William then bestows arms on Harold.

According to the historians, however, Conan was never inside Dol but was actually besieging it when William arrived.[71] There is no reason to suppose that Rennes was besieged, and the Tapestry is the only source for the surrender of the keys of Dinan. The gift

of arms by William to Harold put the English earl in a position of vassalage to William and although it is likely that such an idea had not yet taken root in England, it would be clear to Harold what was happening. There is no mention of any such ceremony in either William of Poitiers' or William of Jumièges' accounts, but both mention gifts to Harold. This scene might thus be a piece of *ex post facto* interpretation by the designer of the Tapestry.

In pl. 21 it will be seen that weapons for the first time penetrate the border of the Tapestry. From this

24-27 William takes Harold to Bayeux, and Harold swears an oath in the presence of William who sits in majesty, holding his sword as a sword of state (the sword, however, being sheathed). Harold then returns by ship to England and sets out to meet Edward.

The oath was seen by both the chroniclers and the designer of the Tapestry as one of the high points of the story. William of Poitiers says that the ceremony took place before the Breton expedition and in this disagrees with the Tapestry. Whether the ceremony took place at Bayeux, as the Tapestry implies, or at

Bonneville-sur-Touques as recorded by William of Poitiers[73] is immaterial; the event became central in Norman eyes.

Harold is seen swearing his oath on two house-shaped reliquaries of a type familiar in the early medieval period.[74] The Tapestry might indicate that it took place out of doors, as the shrines and Harold stand on a representation of a cobbled surface of a form used to represent open ground throughout this part of the Tapestry.

The oblique lines in the border below the largest

tentative beginning the artist is more willing to allow such an invasion of space in order to heighten tension (cf. pl. 23), perhaps the only sign in the Tapestry of a development of the artist's confidence. Conan's flight down a rope from Dol is paralleled by a similar representation in the Old English Hexateuch.[72] The strange feature to the left of the structure on the top of the mound at Dol has not been satisfactorily explained: could it be flames? It is to be noted that neither Dol nor Rennes has any apparent garrison, whereas at Dinan a proper siege is taking place: the

wooden structure is being set on fire and spears are being thrown by both sides.

The two ribbons at William's neck can perhaps be related to the similar ribbons he wears in his civil dress in pl. 15. It is interesting to compare the shields in pl. 21 with that of the man on the rear horse in pl. 20. In the latter the complicated method of holding the shield is clearly shown; in the former a simple loop is all that is indicated.

reliquary unusually sprout vegetal ornament. The ship on which Harold returns to England has the broken gunwale line noted below (page 226), but the sail is treated rather differently from those in pls. 5 and 6, the folds being completely linear and not worked in different coloured strips. The lookout on the English shore stands on an elaborate balcony and curious faces peer out from the windows of the tower behind him. It is not known where Harold landed on his return to England.

Two more fables appear, this time in the upper

borders. One, above the lookout in pl. 27, has been explained as the gander and the cygnet,[75] but this seems most unlikely; it must be a repeat of the crane removing a bone from the wolf's throat as seen in pl. 5. To the right of pl. 27 is yet another version of the crow, the fox and the cheese.[76]

28

29

28–31 Harold comes to Edward, who sits informally on a stool, crowned, but holding a walking stick to emphasize his age. Harold approaches with bowed head, as though seeking a favour, followed by a man bearing an axe. The next three scenes must be taken together. Time has passed: it is now late 1065 and Westminster Abbey is nearly ready for consecration (symbolized by the man putting the final touch to the structure, erecting the weathercock on the east end). In pl. 30 Edward is dying in what is possibly an upper room of his palace at Westminster on 5 January, the

day after the consecration of the Abbey (the consecration symbolized by the Hand of God above the nave). With him are his wife, Harold, a servant and a cleric. His finger touches that of Harold, symbolic of his bequest of the kingdom. Below, Edward is wrapped in his shroud and, to the left, is carried in procession on a bier to be buried in the Abbey, accompanied by boys carrying hand-bells and a group of tonsured clerics. In pl. 31 the crown is offered to Harold as he is told of the death of the king.

Brooks and Walker say that the scene of Harold

32

31–34 Harold enthroned with a crown, orb and sceptre is described as king of the English; Stigand, the archbishop of Canterbury, is beside him, robed and holding a maniple. One of the two figures to the left carries the unsheathed sword of state. To the right a group of figures draws attention to another body of men who 'admire' Halley's comet. The comet – which re-appears every 75–77 years – would have been clearly visible in England 24–30 April 1066; it disappeared from sight in mid-May. Next, a messenger talks to Harold, who inclines towards him as

though listening to secret intelligence. The presence of the outlined ships in the lower border may indicate that the message concerns William's order to build an invasion fleet (it will be noticed that they are not rigged). In that case we have another inverted scene, as this is followed by an English ship arriving in Normandy, presumably bringing to Duke William the news of Harold's accession. The man who wades ashore with the anchor has a Norman hair-style. Gibbs-Smith, however, sees the ships in the border as a ghostly omen seen by Harold in his imagination

and Edward is admonitory, reflecting Eadmer: 'Did I not tell you that I knew William and that your going might bring untold calamity on the kingdom?'[77] The reversal of the death and burial scenes is interpreted by many as emphasizing the hurried nature of the accession.[78] The death scene is reminiscent of that described in the *Vita Ædwardi* (see p. 198) in which Edward places the care of the kingdom and his wife in Harold's hands.

Unusually in pl. 30 the border is breached by the inscription. In pl. 28 Edward wears a square brooch,

perhaps the form worn only by the upper crust (cf. pls. 10 and 31). The shrouded corpse is very close in appearance to corpses in the Old English Hexateuch;[79] the bed is also paralleled in this manuscript, even to the curtain looped round an animal-head post.[80] The crown to the left in pl. 31 is a simple gold cap, not at all like that shown in the coronation scene.

There is a join in the linen of the Tapestry in pl. 30, through the body of the kneeling man.

as a punishment for accepting the throne after his oath to support William's claim'.[81]

Stenton holds that pl. 31 is a scene of acclamation, not coronation,[82] and he believes that Harold is portrayed in Westminster Abbey, where, according to Baldwin of Bury, the coronation took place. Archbishop Stigand of Canterbury, according to William of Poitiers, performed the ceremony, 'an unholy consecration', for Stigand 'had been deprived of his ministry by the justified favour of papal anathema'.[83] This has caused Stenton and others[84] to flirt with the

idea that this scene is Norman propaganda and consequently to support Florence of Worcester's claim that Ealdred, Archbishop of York, performed the ceremony. An unlikely thesis.

The man in the upper border in pl. 33 has been given an Aesopian interpretation by Herrmann.[85] The ship in pl. 33, although quite elaborate with animal-head prow and stern posts and pennant at its mast-head, has an unbroken gunwale and no shields lining its sides, unlike the previously portrayed ships (save those in the border of pl. 32).

34–37 The news of Harold's accession is brought to William, who orders ships to be built. William sits in his hall with a tonsured clerical advisor, presumably his half-brother Odo, Bishop of Bayeux, who gestures to a shipwright carrying a T-shaped axe. Trees are cut down, planks split and ships built and launched ready for the invasion of England.

The shipbuilding scenes are of utmost importance for an understanding of the use of tools in the early medieval period. First the trees are felled with long-hafted symmetrical, straight-bladed felling-axes. A haft of up to a metre in length is ideal for such a

purpose and this is the type of axe depicted here. It would also seem that the branches were trimmed before the tree was felled. Axe-heads of this form are known from early medieval sites, but not complete axes.[86] The planks were presumably split with wedges and then smoothed and shaped (as here) with T-shaped side-axes of a type well known at this period,[87] which may have been in some cases asymmetrical. The broad blade allows a long shaving to be taken from the plank. An interesting detail of the process of plank-trimming is the wedging of the rough plank in a split tree-trunk for ease of working

38–41 The ships having been launched, they are loaded with weapons and provisions, including wine and food. William rides down to the ships, embarks on a large vessel (which seems to have been called the *Mora*[91]) and the fleet sets sail on the night of 27/28 September 1066, the vessels filled with men and horses.

These scenes reveal much about the daily life of the period. Here, for example, is a four-wheeled wagon with framed sides drawn by two men. Though two-

wheeled carts with similar sides are pictured in late Anglo-Saxon manuscripts (in one case, for example, drawn by mules[92] and in another with empty shafts[93]), four-wheeled wagons are rare. The men who draw the wagon use ropes attached by a shackle to what appears to be the seating of two shafts. The felloes of the wheels are clearly indicated. In the wagon are a barrel and weapons. The barrel is long and has a bung in both heads; another barrel of similar form with a single bung is carried on a man's

(pl. 36). Notice also the stacks of timber. A side-axe[88] is being used by the man standing inside the boat in pl. 36 and a T-shaped smoothing-axe by the man inside the upper boat. Another man in the upper boat uses a breast-auger, presumably with a spoon-bit of a type found in many early medieval contexts.[89] The man to the left in the lower boat is perhaps using a hammer. Note that no adzes are being used in these scenes. Both craftsmen in the lower boat have long beards, perhaps a sign of the age and experience necessary in a shipwright.

The ships are built on land (pl. 37), drawn into the sea by ropes tied to their prows, and fastened to a pole in the water. One of the ship's stems (pl. 37) has a hole for the painter (mooring rope), a feature paralleled on an eleventh-century stem from Skuldelev, Denmark. This hole might, however, have been bored specifically for launching.[90] Note that some of the ships have animal-head prows and that there is no break in the gunwales.

From this point forward there is less attempt to differentiate Normans by their hair-style.

shoulder. The elongated form of these barrels is perhaps best paralleled at Hedeby in north Germany in a roughly contemporary context, where a barrel was used as a well lining.[94] Other men carry a sack or bundle (pl. 39) and a dead pig (pl. 38). The cart is filled with spears, all with barbed tips and with crosspieces below the heads. Helmets are placed on the ends of the upright posts which form the sides of the cart. Other men carry weapons, helmets, bundles of swords and mail shirts – the latter carried on poles between two men. The mail shirts look less trousered here than when worn. The method of carrying the mail shirts on poles indicates that they were heavy and made of iron, a fact reflected in a story concerning William's strength in carrying two mail shirts in a foray before Hastings, told by William of Poitiers.[95]

The linen of the Tapestry is joined (as is clearly seen) where there is a minimum of embroidery – between the man carrying the sack and the rearmost rider in pl. 39.

41

42

41–44 The ships cross the Channel and land at Pevensey on 28 September 1066. The masts are lowered, the horses disembarked and the ships, with the aid of a fork-ended pole, are beached.

The ships are formulaic: some have oar-holes, some do not; some have animal-head stem and stern posts, some do not; some have shields lining the side, others do not. Some have pennants at the mast-head; one, perhaps the *Mora*, has an elaborate cruci-

form structure topped by a cross at the mast-head. The steersman often holds the clews of the sails, possibly a depiction of the sheets fastened in the way known as *aktaumar* in later Norse sources.[96]

The ship with the cruciform frame at the mast-head is presumably William's ship, which might account also for the man with the blast-horn at the stem. William of Poitiers' account of the voyage perhaps illuminates the scene:

45

46

44–47 The Normans make an unopposed landing and ride to Hastings and forage in the surrounding country. They slaughter sheep (pl. 45) and bring in food to prepare a feast.

It is clear from the Tapestry that Hastings was the base camp of William's forces and that once they were established there they were able to live off the country while they waited for the arrival of Harold's

army. William of Poitiers says that they fortified Pevensey,[98] but this is only mentioned fleetingly in the Tapestry. To the left in pl. 46 a mounted figure is named as Wadard, a man identified in Domesday Book as a major tenant of Odo, Bishop of Bayeux. His name is rare and the equation can be safely made.

Pl. 46 provides us with a rare view of a pack-animal – a pony – with a pack-saddle. On the left of the same

186

HIC EXEVNT:CABALLI   DENAVIBVS:· ET HIC:MILITES:

43

Fearing lest they reach the opposite shore before daybreak and so incur danger in a hostile and unknown anchorage, the duke issued verbal orders that as soon as they gained the high sea the ships were to lie at anchor close to him for part of the night, until they should see a lantern lit at his masthead, and then at the sound of a trumpet at once set course.[97]

In the lower border in pl. 41 a dog is chasing what appears to be a hare or rabbit (rabbits were introduced into England by the Normans).

44

The fact that the text of the Tapestry mentions the disembarkation of horses may mean that there was something unusual about this idea in the designer's mind. For the disembarkation of horses from the ships, see p.227. It will be noticed that none of the beached ships has ornamental posts at stem and stern. Could it be that they were dismountable?

AD AR D: HIC:COQVI TVR:CARO   ET HIC: MINISTRAVERVN MINISTRI   HIC FECERVN:PRANDIVM:

47

plate, a man carries a pig, whilst on the extreme right of pl. 45 another man carries a circular coil which has been discussed (because of its manuscript parallels) on a number of occasions, particularly by Wormald.[99]

A feast is prepared in the open air; a fowl, kebab-like chunks of meat and single pieces of meat are prepared on spits. A cauldron boils on a fire, possibly in a brazier (pl. 47), and a bearded servant places

cooked food from a stove on a dish. Other men pass food to servants working at a table improvised from a number of shields and a blast-horn summons the guests to table.

The join in the linen base of the Tapestry may be clearly seen to the right of the tower in the middle of pl. 47.

48
49

48–51 The open-air feast is blessed by Bishop Odo. William and his half-brothers sit in council, William holding his sword point uppermost. An order is given to fortify Hastings and workmen, quarrelling on the way, set to work, apparently building a motte. William is told about Harold's approach, a house is fired and a woman and a boy either flee from the house or are caught within it.[100]

The food has been removed from the spit before being brought to the table. The servant below the table carrying a bowl and napkin (presumably for rinsing the fingers) is paralleled in general form in the Old English Hexateuch.[101] The similarity of this scene to the generality of scenes of the Last Supper has been much commented on.[102]

In the building scenes of pls. 49–50, spades, shovels and a mattock are seen. The spades have shoulders on one side and a pointed shoe. The shovels have oval or sub-triangular blades and no shoe. Although spade shoes are occasionally found in Anglo-Saxon contexts,[103] and are illustrated in the manuscripts,[104] Morris has pointed out that triangular-bladed spades are otherwise not found before the thirteenth century.[105] Shovels are unknown in English contexts but a number of ninth-century wooden shovels were found in the Norwegian Oseberg mound, together with some unshod spades.[106]

52

51–54 14 October 1066. William, standing outside the gates of Hastings, prepares to mount his charger, which is held by a groom. He is identified by the ribbons at his neck (cf. pls. 15 and 24). He holds a lance with a pennant below its head. The mounted soldiers gather speed as they ride out to meet Harold in battle. There are no foot soldiers in these scenes; the riders must therefore be seen as the elite of the Norman army. Two soldiers carry pennants or gonfanons on their lances.

The upper border has some odd scenes. In the middle of pl. 52 two naked figures are gesturing at each other; one (a man) holds an axe and an unidentified object, perhaps a bucket. The other, of indeterminate

50

51

The building of a fortification at Hastings is mentioned by William of Poitiers and the position of the element *ceastra* above the motte has led to speculation that this might be a label for the fortification itself. The occurrence of the name *Hestengaceastra* is, however, too common to accept this. It might be intended by the artist both as a label and as part of the name (see note 40, p. 229).

The ravaging of the countryside, indicated by the burning of the house in pl. 50, is recorded by William of Poitiers, who says that it was one of the reasons why Harold speeded up his march south.[107] This in itself was a tactical error, for Harold had everything to gain by delay as William had to live on an inhospitable countryside.

As far as pl. 48 the inscription has been executed in black or very dark green letters. The letters are now alternately sage green and terracotta (although the earlier colour does reappear occasionally, e.g. pl. 61 and 69).

The top element of the letter T in AT (pl. 49) is not illustrated in de Montfaucon, nor is the A in the element HESTENGA.[108]

53

54

sex, but possibly a woman, holds out her arms towards him. On very slender grounds this has been identified as the fable of the widow and the soldier.[109] The scene to the left in pl. 53 shows a naked man (probably an Englishman, as he has a moustache) making sexual advances to a naked woman, whose breasts and pubic hair are clearly visible.[110] The two animals next in the border have been identified as illustrating the story of the ass and the wolf,[111] but this identification is extremely tenuous.

There is a join in the linen to the left of the letter A of AD in pl. 53. It can best be seen below the hindquarters of the blue horse.

55

54–56 William enquires of Vital about the position of the English army and a fully armed Harold is told about the position of William's army.

William holds a club and behind him is either Odo or Robert with a mace. Vital comes towards him holding a lance, probably riding from the hill to the right where Norman scouts have observed Harold's army. Vital has been identified from Domesday Book as a tenant of Bishop Odo and as Vitalis de Cantebrie in an eleventh-century inquisition of St Augustine's, Canterbury.[112] This is a crucial scene as many sources agree that Harold wished to take William by surprise,

57   58

57–60 William, now bearing a club, encourages his troops and they set out for the battle. For the first time we see unmounted Norman soldiers (pl. 60, right). William's speech is reconstructed in heroic form from William of Poitiers' imagination.[115] It is interesting to see how the artist gives an impression of gathering momentum throughout this sequence.

Both the lower and upper borders include various scenes which have been identified with fables. In pl. 57, for example (bottom right), an animal stands in front of a group of animals in a cave, whilst a spotted animal carries off a bird in pl. 59.[116]

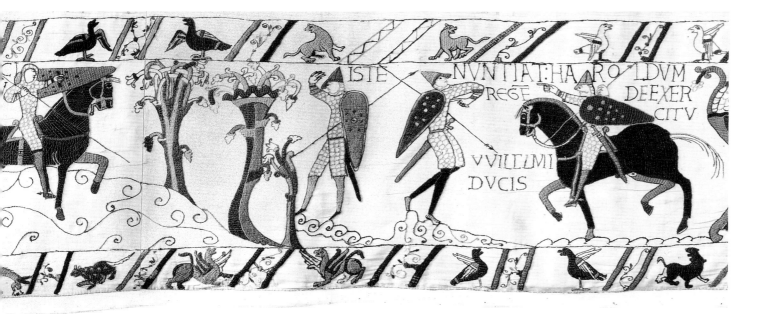

56

but was foiled by William's scouts who, according to local tradition, saw the English on Battle Ridge from Telham Hill two miles away.[113] Indeed it seems that Harold was himself, if not surprised, caught in disarray. The English lookouts, unlike the Normans, are on foot.

The hawk hunting the hare to the extreme left in the lower border of pl. 54, and the ass and the animal to its right in the lower border of pl. 55, have been assigned unconvincingly to the Aesop cycle.[114] The last animal has even been identified as a weasel – if so, it is a very fat one!

59   **60**

61

60–63 The battle commences. The Norman cavalry, backed by archers, charge the English army which consists of unmounted soldiers (including one archer who wears no armour) and which seems to be formed up behind the legendary 'shield-wall'.

In the lower border the dead and dying are mingled with scattered weapons. The Normans attack with lances, bows and arrows and a sword. The English reply in like manner, using spears, bows and arrows and an axe. No attempt is made to differenti-

ate the arms used on either side, but the circular shield in the middle of the lower border of pl. 63 is presumably of English form (see pp. 223–4). Only one sword is being used in these scenes, but it is noteworthy that spears are being used as javelins, many of them being thrown overarm (pl. 61, centre). Some of the spears, such as that of the leading horseman in pl. 61, are couched (i.e. held underarm). It is not without interest that in pl. 61 a mace is seen flying through the air, as though thrown in panic. All the

63–66 The scene of the death of Gyrth and Leofwine starts as three Norman knights ride towards them. Surrounded, they both die. The battle proceeds on its bloody course and the English hold out with difficulty on a hill.

Gyrth, Earl of East Anglia and Oxfordshire, and Leofwine, earl in the area surrounding the eastern Thames from Buckinghamshire and Surrey to Essex, probably fell in the afternoon. Brooks and Walker suggest that both men appear twice in pl. 64, but this is hard to prove.[119]

After the death of Harold's brothers, the artist seems carried away by a mood of excitement and movement. The battle gets fiercer; in pl. 65, for example, an axe is decapitated by a sword, a horse is killed with an axe and swords are wielded with great abandon. Horses tumble onto a spiked defence, and in pl. 66 a soldier is actually holding the end of the girth of a toppling horse, as though pulling it down. Brown[120] has convincingly argued that the scene in pls. 65–66 of the tumbling horses represents the so-called Malfosse episode, following William of Malmesbury who

62

63

weapons piercing the English shields in pl. 61 are arrows, whereas in pl. 62 they are all spears. The whole scene must be interpreted as a conventionalized battle – a fight between the more aristocratic soldiers on each side. They are, with few exceptions, fully armed with mail-shirts and knightly armour. The archer on the English side (pl. 61) is represented on a smaller scale, perhaps indicating that he was a man of minimal importance to the upper-class audience of the Tapestry.

The carnage represented in the lower scene is paralleled in a less blood-curdling form in the slightly earlier Old English Hexateuch, as Abraham pursues Lot's captors.[117] Dead soldiers are, however, rarely seen in Anglo-Saxon art, although in a very bland form they do appear on the Franks' Casket.[118]

The word EXERCITV̄ in pls. 60–61 is worked in a single colour, as was the text in the earlier part of the Tapestry.

66

may well have been basing his narrative on the Tapestry. In this story the Normans were attacking the English, strongly positioned on a hill, and retreated in feigned flight (according to Henry of Huntingdon) into a concealed ditch. A defensive work of sharpened stakes is clearly seen beneath the fallen horses in pl. 65. In most early sources the Malfosse incident is consigned to the end of the battle. It is not without interest that the Normans are here described as *Franci*.

It is noticeable in pl. 66 that the English are not

wearing mail, but, unlike Gyrth and Leofwine in pl. 64, they carry kite-shaped shields. Many of them have prominent moustaches and one (pl. 67) has a beard.

The lower border is filled with dead and dismembered corpses, broken weapons and even a dead horse. The fallen warriors in pl. 66 do not appear in de Montfaucon;[121] the light red wool is a repair, a feature seen in much of the border from this point on.

67

68

67–70 Odo encourages the troops, William shows himself
to his soldiers to deny rumours of his death and the
Normans, reorganizing, continue the battle. Ahead
of the duke, and pointing at him, rides a figure identified in the border above as E . . . TIVS, presumably
Eustace of Boulogne, who is recorded by William of
Poitiers as having been present at the battle. The
scene in which William lifts his helmet is also described by William of Poitiers. The Normans, think-

ing that William was dead, began to flee. William,
however, 'galloped up in front of them, shouting and
brandishing his lance. Removing his helmet to bare
his head, he cried, "Look at me, I am alive, and,. by
God's help, I shall win."'[122]

Eustace carries an elaborate banner which has been
identified as the papal banner described by William
of Poitiers as being carried into battle by the
Normans.[123]

71

72

70–73 Harold within the shield-wall is killed, shot in the eye
by an arrow and hewn in the leg as he lies on the
ground. The English then flee from the battle, hotly
pursued by mounted Normans.

The killing of Harold is one of the scenes in the
Tapestry most difficult of interpretation. Brooks and
Walker[124] argue that Harold is indeed killed by an
arrow in his eye but that he is shown again lying on
the ground being cut in the leg by a sword (pl. 71).
They argue against Gibbs-Smith,[125] who sees Harold
simply as the latter figure. The Tapestry is the earliest
source for the arrow story and Brooks and Walker's

interpretation is almost certainly right. William of
Malmesbury, possibly deriving his story from the
Tapestry, states that Harold was struck on the thigh
by a Norman knight after being struck by the arrow.
Attempts have been made to reconstruct an arrow in
the eye of the fallen warrior,[126] where there are needle holes. But these holes are not shown by de Montfaucon, Stothard or Sansonetti – all, particularly
Stothard, being accurate observers of stitch-marks.
This is one of the few places where stitch-marks have
not been reconstructed in the Tapestry and, as there
is no place where they are more obvious, they are

69
70

In pl. 70 a strange oval shield might be a perspective rendering of a circular English shield. The rider who strikes the man with this shield has moved out of the saddle and sits on the neck of the horse. This presumably refers to an event in the battle known to the audience, but not recorded in the surviving histories. In the lower border is an army of Norman archers (much restored), none of whom is dressed in armour. In pl. 69 the quivers of the archers are much

exaggerated in size. Odo in pl. 67 carries what is described as a *baculum*, which he seems to be holding with some relish. He is not dressed in armour, but wears a helmet. For the word *baculum*, see p. 225. William's club (pl. 68) is a much rougher instrument.

The linen is joined in pl. 68 under the hindquarters of the blue horse in front of Eustace and between the letters C and F.

73

presumably a fabrication of the last century. The arrow in the eye of the standing Harold is a restoration from stitch-marks seen by both Stothard and de Montfaucon; the other stitch-marks could not have escaped the early restorer's hand.

The last three plates are much restored, but full of detail. The borders portray dismembered bodies, archers, the looting of the dead and even quarrelling looters (pl. 71, right). At one place (left in pl. 71) one of the animals typically found in the border has escaped into the main field, the only such occurrence in the whole hanging.

The end of the Tapestry may not be complete but what survives is certainly lively – riding men with whips hunt the fleeing Englishmen, one of whom looks apprehensively over his shoulder. Three of the Englishmen carry maces and one appears to be withdrawing an arrow from his eye.

The final part of the inscription ET FVGA VERTERUNT ANGLI has been restored (as have many of the figures) since de Montfaucon reproduced the Tapestry, although it was dotted in by Stothard.[127]

195

Fig. 1 Detail of the back of the Tapestry, photographed during cleaning and remounting in 1982–3 (see pls. 51, 52).

III The Story Told in the Tapestry

THE FIRST PORTION of the Tapestry (pls. 1–26) recounts a journey made by Harold to Normandy, a journey which culminated in a vow of obligation by Harold to William. Contemporary English accounts do not record this visit, but William of Poitiers' record suggests that it was in late 1063 or in 1064. The Anglo-Saxon Chronicle is completely blank in all its versions for 1064, and as Harold was apparently fighting the Welsh until the late summer of 1063 it is almost certain that the events retailed by the Tapestry started in the spring of 1064. The first scene shows an enthroned Edward, apparently giving instructions to Harold. Harold leaves the king and goes to Bosham where, after praying and feasting, he takes ship and lands in Ponthieu. Both William of Jumièges and William of Poitiers – writing, it must be emphasized, after the Conquest – state that Harold was asked to go to Normandy by Edward in order to confirm the succession of the English crown to William, but the Tapestry gives no indication of the reason for the journey. William of Poitiers also states that Edward 'felt the hour of his death approaching'.

Another source suggests another reason for the journey. Eadmer's *Historia Novorum in Anglia* (written by an Englishman between 1110 and 1143) states that Harold had persuaded a reluctant Edward to allow him to go to Normandy. The purpose of the journey was to bring back his brother Wulfnoth and his nephew Hakon, who were William's hostages.[128] But, as Harold seems to have been singularly lacking in charity to his brothers and the rest of the family, Eadmer's rather daft story seems unlikely.

It was extremely foolhardy of Harold to go to Normandy, even if he was ordered to do so, and both Freeman and Stenton have suggested that he was going elsewhere, was blown off course and fell into Norman hands.[129] What then seems to be the most likely reason for this journey? The version expressed by William of Poitiers, although marginally the most likely, smacks of Norman propaganda. Against it one might argue, first, that in 1064 Edward, if old, was hale and hearty and hardly contemplating death (Harold was expecting him to hunt in Wales as late as 1065[130] – not the activity of a frail man). Second, Harold was probably already a serious contender for succession to the throne and one might reasonably question whether Edward had the political strength to order an ambitious man fresh from his successes in battle in Wales – one of the most powerful and ruthless men in the kingdom – to promise the throne to a bastard foreign count. The accident theory might just be hinted at in the Tapestry in that Harold embarks accompanied by hunting dogs and a hawk (pl. 4) with no panoply of armour and no horses, and is seized unarmed by Guy of Ponthieu on a beach outside William's dominions (pl. 7). It is at least possible that he was setting off on a long-distance hunting trip on his estates in Wales or elsewhere, or even on a visit to friends of the English royal family, the counts of Flanders.[131] Is it possible that we have here a double meaning – one intended for a Norman audience and an entirely different one intended for an English audience? The Tapestry, often so explicit in its text, does not say (as does William of Poitiers) that Edward *sent* Harold anywhere; the implication could equally be that Harold was merely taking leave of the king before retiring to his estates, one of which happened to be Bosham (pl. 3) on the south coast. Brooks and Walker[132] have reaffirmed the opinion that the idea that Edward sent Harold to Normandy to announce the succession was a vital element in the Norman claims to the English crown and that the Tapestry designer may have been hinting at English versions of this event.

On landing in France, Harold is seized by Count Guy of Ponthieu and taken to Beaurain. William hears of Harold's arrival in Ponthieu and sends messengers to bring him to Rouen. Both William of Jumièges and William of Poitiers describe these events in lesser or greater detail, both agree that Guy seized Harold and threw him into prison. The two chroniclers may well have exaggerated the events to give an impression of William's power and influence in obtaining the release of the captive, for the Tapestry does not suggest this and indeed common sense would suggest that such an important prisoner would be treated with respect. The Tapestry shows the seizure, but Harold is clearly conducted with great ceremony, carrying his hawk and accompanied by his dogs to Guy's residence. The honour with which Harold is shown to have been treated in the Tapestry is further strengthened by the fact that William rides out to greet him and to escort him to his palace (pls. 15–16), where, according to William of Poitiers, Harold was received hospitably.

The episode of the priest and Ælfgyva acts as a break in the narrative at this point, but is followed by William and Harold setting out on a campaign against Duke Conan of Brittany, who escapes from Dol, but is ultimately captured after the siege of

Dinan. The campaign in Brittany is mentioned by William of Poitiers, who is (with the Tapestry) the chief source for this particular episode in the chaotic history of the province. William was called in by Breton rebels, notably Riwallon of Dol. William answered their call, defeated Conan, but withdrew leaving Conan still in charge, free to send Riwallon into exile. Basically William had invaded Brittany to demonstrate his power, protect his flank and build up a party which supported Normandy in Conan's territory. Whether deliberate or not, this attack stood William in good stead when he invaded England in 1066, for he was able to take a Breton contingent with him whilst Conan was busy seeking alliances elsewhere and attacking Anjou instead of Normandy.[133] There are thus a number of ideas behind these scenes; William is portrayed as a brave warrior and so is Harold. They are seen acting together with William as the leader and Harold as a subordinate and the scene is set for Harold's great act of treachery as seen through Norman eyes. Having eaten William's salt it would be almost obligatory within the canons of heroic behaviour required at the time for Harold to fight for his host, and it might not be too much to suggest that William was subtle enough to see that Harold would have to acknowledge him as his lord after such a campaign.

We now come to one of the cruces of the Tapestry. Harold receives arms from William on the field of battle and Harold and William return to Bayeux, 'Where', in the words of the Tapestry, 'Harold made a sacred oath to William' (pls. 25–26). The Norman chroniclers make much of this, particularly William of Poitiers, who places the event at Bonneville-sur-Touques before the Breton campaign. It is worth quoting this account *in extenso*:

Harold publicly swore fealty to him by the sacred rite of Christians. And according to the entirely truthful relation of certain most notable men of utter integrity who were present at the time, at the end of the oath he freely added the following clauses: that he would be the agent (*vicarius*) of duke William at the court of his lord king Edward as long as the latter lived; that he would strive with all his influence and power to bring about the succession of the English kingdom to William after Edward's death; that he would meanwhile hand over to the custody of William's knights the fortress at Dover at his own expense and also that he would place in the keeping of the duke's agents other fortresses, abundantly supplied, in various parts of the kingdom where the duke should require them to be raised. The duke, having accepted Harold as his vassal by homage (*jam satelliti suo accepto per manus*), at Harold's request, before the oath, confirmed him with all his lands and powers (*terras ejus cunctumque potentum dedit petenti*). Indeed it was not expected that Edward, already ill, would live much longer.[134]

This oath was central to William's claim and there can be little doubt that an agreement in the vein of that outlined by William of Poitiers was sworn. William's motives are clear: he wanted to establish his right to the throne of England. Harold's are obscure. Eadmer and other apologists have suggested that

Harold acted under duress or was tricked into taking the oath. He was clearly in a difficult position. He was in a foreign – hostile – country and he had just been fighting for William in a subordinate capacity. William of Poitiers' account is clearly written *ex post facto*, for the third and fourth conditions of the oath (as Stenton has pointed out[135]) might have been treasonable against Edward. It may be that Harold felt that he could easily repudiate the oath at a later date, pleading that it had been taken under duress. We may never know, but it is clear that to the Normans this was a crucial act, one which in Norman eyes was more important than the later coronation or acclamation of Harold. Indeed the sacred elements of the coronation of Harold are not represented in the Tapestry. There is merely a statement which recognizes him as king: *Hic residet Harold rex Anglorum* (pl. 31), which is awkward to translate. Perhaps it should be rendered 'here sits *enthroned* Harold King of the English' rather than merely 'here sits Harold . . .', but to this we shall return. To most scholars the oath-taking is the central point of the story told by the Tapestry.

After the oath-taking Harold is seen returning to England, meeting Edward and possibly being admonished by him – Harold almost seems to be cringing in pl. 28. Then we have the inversion of Edward's funeral and his deathbed, followed by the accession of Harold to the throne, crowned, orbed and sceptred. The Norman sources are relatively silent about these affairs. The death of Edward as it appears in the Tapestry is close in many ways to the story as told in the *Vita Ædwardi*. Edward is shown in the Tapestry as dying in the presence of his queen, Harold, the archbishop and others:

And stretching forth his hand to . . . Harold he said, 'I commend this woman and all the kingdom to your protection. Serve and honour her with faithful obedience as your Lady and sister, which she is, and do not despoil her, as long as she lives, of any due honour got from me. Likewise I commend those men who have left their native land for love of me, and have up till now served me faithfully. Take from them an oath of fealty, if they should so wish, or send them with your safe conduct safely across the Channel to their houses with all that they acquired from me . . .'[136]

In the Tapestry we see the king stretching out his hand towards Harold, as though appointing him his successor. It may well be that the *Vita* and the Tapestry were using the same source. Edward died in London on 5 January 1066 and was buried the next day before the high altar of the new Westminster Abbey, which was his greatest memorial. Harold was immediately crowned in the Abbey and the legitimacy of his position is recognized by his title *rex* in the Tapestry. Archbishop Stigand is present in the accession scene of the Tapestry.

Following this, Halley's comet is seen in the sky and the news of Harold's accession is brought to William, who orders a fleet to be built and provisioned for the invasion. There is no mention of the hectic events in England as first Harold's brother Tostig and then Harald of Norway attempted to invade the country and were dealt with by the king. From now on (pls. 33ff.) the Tapestry tells the story of William of Normandy and of the conquest of England. The political manoeuvrings are not all, however, illuminated by the Tapestry; for William, we know from other sources, was very active. He held councils, gained allies and tried to secure his Norman base through his wife and his son Robert. The church was bolstered in Normandy and (in an attempt to justify his cause) he appealed to the pope, although nothing is known of the grounds on which this appeal was made. Pope Alexander II, however, publicly proclaimed his support of William's English enterprise. The young emperor, Henry IV, also gave his approval, and French and Flemish support was canvassed. The fleet, as shown in the Tapestry, was constructed and prepared for sea at the mouth of the Dives. The fleet was much delayed by contrary winds but early in September it was moved to the Somme in preparation for the invasion. At about the same time Harold had been compelled to dismiss his defensive forces because of lack of provisions and money.[137] On 27 September at nightfall the fleet set sail and William with all his troops landed at Pevensey on the following day without opposition – all brilliantly shown in the Tapestry (two days earlier Harold had defeated Harald of Norway at Stamford Bridge in far-off Yorkshire).

The Tapestry now gathers dramatic momentum as events lead up to the Battle of Hastings. The army forages, cooks a feast and throws up a fortification at Hastings; houses are burnt and, as Harold is told of the events, the Normans march from Hastings to give battle. Harold does not appear in this section of the Tapestry; the famous victory of Stamford Bridge and the heroic, if somewhat impetuous, march south by Harold in something like fourteen days is perforce ignored. The Tapestry gives no information concerning Harold's raising of his southern army – nor indeed does it indicate whether he had brought his northern army with him. The Norman sources credit Harold with the plan of taking William by surprise, but this was not to be; William's scouts had spotted his approach.

The Tapestry now portrays the battle. Vital is asked if he has seen the enemy and he is able to indicate the presence of the English, Harold is briefed concerning the situation and William exhorts his followers. Battle is joined, Harold's brothers are killed, Bishop Odo appears, as does Eustace of Boulogne. Harold and his followers are killed and the English are put to flight. Although the Tapestry gives a very spirited rendering of the course of the battle, we must turn for more detailed knowledge of the events to the written sources and particularly to William of

Poitiers. The events of 14 October 1066 start at about 9.00 a.m. with the English being surprised by the Normans on ground not of their own choice. Modern consensus puts the size of each army at about 7000.[138] The Tapestry concentrates, with few exceptions, on the fight between the more important men – the cavalry on the Norman side and the mailed English soldiers.

William was clearly the better general, managing to fight on ground of his choosing; initially, however, Harold was able to draw his troops up on the ridge above the settlement later to be known as Battle. To the south William drew up his army in three lines at the foot of the slope, with his cavalry as the rearmost line. William was in the centre, presumably with his Normans; William of Poitiers says that the Bretons were on the left. Duke William commanded an army of cavalry and infantry, the English had no cavalry. The English infantry stood firm against an uphill attack by the Normans, first with their infantry and then with their mounted soldiers. Part of William's army (the Bretons) started to retreat, their distress fuelled by a rumour that William had been killed. William, as is graphically illustrated on the Tapestry (pl. 68), showed himself to disprove the rumour and rallied his troops, leading an attack to decimate those English who had been foolishly drawn downhill by the retreating Normans.

Battle was resumed but the English stood firm until, as William of Poitiers says, the Normans feigned flight and lured the English to follow them downhill, so that they might fight on more equal terms. The Tapestry does not show this. There is no need to doubt the Normans' ability to produce the discipline to feign this retreat and even to do it again; Brown, who is a strong supporter of the accuracy of William of Poitiers' statement, has argued that the retreat might have been carried out with strict discipline by small units used to fighting together.[139] The Tapestry continues the story, showing first the death of Harold's brothers, Gyrth and Leofwine, but the retreat may be indicated by the scene (pls. 66–67) where the English are surrounded on a hill. If this is so, the situation is reversed from the sequence of events described by William of Poitiers, for Duke William is seen identifying himself in the scene which immediately follows. The Tapestry then shows the troops attacking Harold's bodyguards and this scene is followed by another of the dramatic highlights of the Tapestry – the death of Harold.

The Tapestry is the only primary source for the manner of Harold's death; William of Poitiers does not go into detail and William of Jumièges' description is muddled and erroneous, merely recording that Harold died at the start of the battle covered with many wounds.[140] There is no doubt that the Tapestry depicts the arrow in Harold's eye. The arrow has in fact been re-embroidered, but Stothard's engraving shows dotted indications of its presence.[141] It is generally agreed that Harold is also shown in the next scene lying on the ground, being rather unsportingly cut about the leg by a mounted soldier.[142] This interpretation of the scene is probably correct, particularly as William of Malmesbury seems to imply some such blow in his much later account of the battle.[143] Recent investigation of both the back and front of the Tapestry by David Bernstein shows a line of seventeen stitch-holes which in size, spacing and condition would suggest that there was originally an arrow in the eye of the fallen figure.[144] I reserve judgment concerning these needle holes. They are not indicated in Stothard's engraving, which is usually very accurate and so would almost certainly have been shown by him. Could they be a later addition?

The account of the battle is now best left to William of Poitiers:

Evening was now falling, and the English clearly saw that they could not hold out much longer against the Normans. They knew they had lost a great part of their army, and that their king with two of his brothers and many of their greatest men had fallen. Those who still stood were almost exhausted, and they realised that they could expect no more help. They saw the Normans, not much diminished by casualties, threatening them with even greater fury than at the beginning of the battle, as if the fighting had actually increased their vigour. They saw the implacable fury of the duke who spared none who came against him and whose prowess could not rest until victory was won. They, therefore, began to fly as swiftly as they could, some on looted horses, some on foot, some along the roads, many over the open country. Those who struggled but on rising lacked the strength to flee lay in their own blood. Others, although disabled, were given strength to move by fear. Many left their corpses in the depths of the forest, and others were found by their pursuers lying by the roadside. Although ignorant of the countryside the Normans eagerly carried on the pursuit, and slaughtering their fleeing opponents brought a fitting end to this victory, while the hooves of the horses exacted punishment from the dead they rode upon.[145]

The Tapestry ends at this point although it is likely that other scenes have been lost: Gibbs-Smith expresses the feelings of many in suggesting that (although it would not have been much longer) the Tapestry would have been completed as it had begun, with a throned king, William, to balance Edward the Confessor who appears throned in the first scene.[146]

One final comment on the direct narrative of the Tapestry concerns the story, recorded in William of Poitiers and Odericus Vitalis, which tells how in the course of the pursuit of the English the Normans rode furiously into a deep ditch or ravine – the *Malfosse* – in badly broken ground.[147] Allen Brown has tentatively suggested that the scene of tumbling horses (pls. 65–66) is a representation of this incident, but his alternative version, that it represents part of the feigned flight, seems to be more likely in view of its position on the Tapestry.

IV   Style, Art and Form

The analysis of a unique work of art in a rarely surviving material cannot be lightly entered upon. The drawing of art-historical parallels is difficult and laboured if not impossible, but certain elements of style and motif are readily identifiable and parallels can be drawn with individual features. But in grand conception there is no clear parallel, no prototype, no model, for the Bayeux Tapestry: no tapestry or any manuscript of the period illustrates by drawings historical events of the recent past. That such hangings were produced by the Anglo-Saxons is known from a single record, about which rather too much has been made. Ælflæd, widow of Byrhtnoth, ealdorman of Essex, presented to the church at Ely a hanging, commissioned after his death at the Battle of Maldon in 991, recording her husband's probity and as a memorial to him.[148] How common such hangings were cannot be said, but this might have been a traditional way of recording great deeds. In the case of the Byrhtnoth hanging there seems to have been some element of a cult of a hero, in that Ely had claimed his body and received a tapestry. Indeed it is arguable from the text (*cortinam gestis viri sui intextam atque depictam in memoriam probitatis eius*) that it may not have shown any of his military deeds – merely his good works – although Byrhtnoth elsewhere is celebrated as an heroic warrior (see below, p. 203). The source, the *Liber Eliensis,* is late and it is impossible to say what had been added to the narrative in the centuries since the event it describes or whether the hanging then at Ely was of earlier or later date than the death of Byrhtnoth. Further, its size or shape are not recorded.

The idea of textile hangings was of course familiar in ecclesiastical contexts in England from the seventh century onwards, and in the late twelfth century there is even a wall-painting of a figured tapestry at Corhampton, Hampshire, which is most unsatisfactorily published. Secular hangings are encountered in wills, poetry and descriptive texts,[149] but whether these hangings were figured or not is often unclear from the text. Raymond Page and Catherine Hills have for example questioned this in relation to the hangings (*web*) described in *Beowulf*.[150] Figured hangings are sometimes mentioned, but what is clear is that in ecclesiastical and other texts, as in *Beowulf*, the sumptuousness of the hangings is commented upon with some frequency: gold, purple and silk are all mentioned.[151] It is this which leads Dodwell to comment, 'the Bayeux Tapestry would have been consi-

dered quite ordinary by the Anglo-Saxons, for it lacks the preciousness of gold thread which was one of their hallmarks of excellence'.[152] This seems rather too readily dismissive. The scale of the Bayeux Tapestry is such that to have covered it with gold would be both impossibly expensive and – in relation to manuscript painting of the period for example – not in the latest taste. The hanging described by Baudri de Bourgueil as adorning the chamber of Adela, William the Conqueror's daughter,[153] used by Dodwell to point his argument, with its silk and gold threads (which features are almost certainly a literary formula) was, if it existed, made of materials that could hardly be considered practicable in a hanging nearly 70 metres long. There is physical evidence, slight but solid, of the quality of English embroidery in the pre-Conquest period, but such remains are few and far between. Some of these textiles were certainly worked in gold, as witness the so-called *casula* of St Harlindis and St Relindis[154] and the stole and maniple of St Cuthbert.[155] But the likelihood of working a hanging of the size of the Bayeux Tapestry in such materials and in such detail is remote.

In this chapter it will become increasingly obvious that I agree with most recent commentators that the Tapestry is English – indeed I have already implied this. But in order to justify such a statement it is necessary briefly to outline the state of art in Normandy, because it is quite possible, and indeed it is generally accepted, that the patron of this work (probably Bishop Odo of Bayeux) was a Norman. The great monastic reform movement in Normandy at the beginning of the eleventh century did not, as in England, make a great deal of impact on the minor arts. Though architecture flourished in Normandy as never before, we read of no startling hangings or textiles, and such manuscript painting as survives had little originality. This is what Michael Kauffmann says of it:

At this period, Norman illumination is characterized by a dependence on Anglo-Saxon art and by a preoccupation with initials to the exclusion or relative absence of major illustrative picture cycles. The Normans were great conquerors, colonizers, builders and administrators, but as far as painting was concerned they lagged far behind their Anglo-Saxon contemporaries. Norman book illumination is permeated with Anglo-Saxon features; indeed to some extent it may be seen as a provincial version of an art at which pre-Conquest England excelled. Yet the Norman artist produced a harder, drier, more solid version of the Anglo-Saxon style and to this extent his art was more Romanesque in character.[156]

England, indeed, had a lively – if sometimes over-ornate – art which had often influenced Normandy before the Conquest, but which had never really been taken over in a pure form in the Duchy. The Conquest led to a total reorganization of the English Church, Norman bishops and monks came to England in profusion and the two cultures were intermixed so as to strengthen and distribute English art in the Duchy as in England. Norman and English scribes and artists worked alongside each other on both sides of the Channel, producing service books for the Norman bishops and monasteries. An Anglo-Norman Romanesque style developed, in which it is quite often difficult to separate English from Norman elements. It is against this background that the Bayeux Tapestry must be seen.

What is it?

The Bayeux Tapestry is a wall hanging, but what was its purpose, from what tradition did it spring and what does it mean? It tells the story of the background of the Battle of Hastings; it tells of William's claims to the throne of England and of Harold taking that throne despite promises to the contrary. It portrays William as a generous man and as a great warrior, it portrays him in other wars in heroic fashion and it treats Harold no less respectfully. It recognizes Harold as king and allows him a glorious and heroic death in battle.

It is, as we have seen, first mentioned in the fifteenth century as being in the cathedral of Bayeux, where it was displayed on the feast of the relics. Its original use is, however, unknown. Two main propositions have been tabled: first, that it was religious in intent; second, that it was secular. Traditionally it was associated with Matilda, William the Conqueror's queen – indeed it is suggested that she herself embroidered it.[157] There is no evidence for this, although the record of this tradition goes back at least to the early eighteenth century.

Fowke[158] was the first to argue convincingly that the patron of the hanging was Odo of Bayeux. The arguments for this are strong. Odo himself is portrayed in an important rôle in the Tapestry and two or possibly three people (Vital, Wadard and perhaps Turold) who are also represented in the hanging have been convincingly shown to have been Odo's retainers – men of some importance. Against this it could be argued that Odo would almost certainly have appeared in the Tapestry whether he was its patron or not, for he was William's half brother – like Robert, Count of Mortain, who is also portrayed on the hanging. Further, as the invasion was backed by the pope, Odo's presence as a churchman might be emphasized to support William's claim. The argument for Odo then rests most securely on two factors: on the names of the retainers and on the fact that the Tapestry is now in Bayeux, the seat of Odo's bishopric – a strong, but not overwhelming, case.

If the Tapestry was intended as a religious document one would point to the centrality of the oath-taking scene (pls. 25–26). This was big magic and is well attested in the contemporary sources as such, being one of the main planks in William's claim. On the other hand the Tapestry also shows – although in an elided form – the coronation of Harold. This was by any standards an important religious act and one which William set aside. If the oath scene is taken as important it would be a fit scene to place with the rest of the story in a religious context. If it were to be part of the secular treasure of the cathedral – *a* cathedral – it would not matter if it had no religious significance or only some religious significance, for we have abundant evidence of secular objects given or left to religious foundations. Francis Wormald argued strongly for the Tapestry being of deep significance with regard to the oath. He stressed the fact that the Tapestry was displayed on the feast of the relics and goes on to say, 'Harold's oath was sworn at Bayeux and was sworn on relics. If indeed Odo did present the Tapestry to his new Cathedral to be shown on the feast of the relics, is it too far-fetched to suggest that in telling the story of Harold and his fall he also wished to convey a warning to those who swear falsely on relics and in particular on the relics of Bayeux?'[159] A very strong argument.

But is it strong enough? The Tapestry celebrates a worldly story. Battles, bloodshed and feasting are perhaps the most immediate impressions one receives from it. The story is heroic and the actors military heroes. Odo of Bayeux was only incidentally a bishop; as Dodwell says, it was 'stark secular ambition which took him from Normandy to England, made him Earl of Kent and William's vicegerent, and induced him to build up great wealth on the spoils of the churches'. For the English, the Tapestry celebrates the downfall and death of their legitimately crowned king (himself a hero figure) and to them the scene with the relics would not seem as important as the slighting of a king crowned with benefit of the Church. Dodwell was the first to suggest – to my mind convincingly – that the Tapestry is a secular object, made for a secular building, perhaps the hall of Bishop Odo.[160]

Dodwell sees a consonance between the Tapestry and the *chanson de geste*, the French epic form of poetry of heroic cast which rejoices in warfare and military action. He particularly draws attention to the fact that most *chansons* encompass treachery and that this is one of the central themes of the Bayeux Tapestry if one believes that the oath-taking is the key to the whole. He draws a sometimes valid, sometimes rather artificial, parallel with the *Chanson de Roland* and with other *chansons* of the Middle Ages. It is, however, difficult to find such a poem before the twelfth century, although it is 'generally considered that they were known in some form in the second half of the eleventh century'. There is, however, another body of poetry which does not have to be assumed at this period, which exists and which like the *chansons de geste* reflects the heroic ideal, namely Old English poetry. Could this provide a literary context for the Bayeux Tapestry?

It is interesting that a recent commentator on Old English poetry should adumbrate the idea that the Battle of Hastings would fit exactly into the mould of Old English poetry.[161] Let us examine this mould, for here may well be the origin of the idea of the Bayeux Tapestry. *Beowulf, The Battle of Maldon*, the *Finnsburh* fragment and parts of *Waldere* are all Old English heroic stories which reflect a tradition far away from the brutal and nasty. The actors in the story act with dignity, thought and honour; they may be on the 'wrong' side, they may win or lose, but they carry through their actions to a fated conclusion with a respect for their beliefs; treachery is not a *sine qua non* of the story, although it does occasionally occur.[162] The poetry encompasses irony and understatement; the poet tends to see both sides of the story and he expects his audience to understand this approach and to blame nobody.

Closest in date to the Bayeux Tapestry is *The Battle of Maldon*.[163] The poem lacks a beginning and (coincidentally like the Bayeux Tapestry) an end; it tells of the defeat of Byrhtnoth, ealdorman of Essex and one of the two or three senior men in England, at the hands of the Scandinavians in 991 (see above, p. 201). Maldon may well have been an important battle, a turning point in the reign of the ill-fated Æthelred; it was certainly important in that it encompassed (as did Hastings) the death of the most important military leader in the country. The poem records how the English led by Byrhtnoth ride to a causeway across the River Blackwater, near Maldon in Essex. Separated from the Scandinavians by the river, Byrhtnoth draws up his troops on the bank. The enemy ask for tribute and this is contemptuously refused. The Vikings can only reach the English across the causeway, but unwisely, as it happened, Byrhtnoth allows them to cross and the battle proceeds amongst speeches of exhortation and descriptions of individual deeds. Byrhtnoth is killed and his loyal followers fight on to the death while others flee in disgrace. The whole is written as a series of vignettes and, of course, relies largely on literary form and direct poetic speech. And yet the parallel to the view of the Battle of Hastings as expressed in the vignette-like quality of the Bayeux Tapestry is clear. Named men die, the leaders are seen in the heat of battle, generals exhort their men, a great soldier is slain and the defeated flee the field. It is of course a familiar image, but none the less it is one which in both cases emphasizes without condemnation a heroic struggle to defeat and to victory, in which certain postures are recollected by the artist and the poet.

If we accept that the Bayeux Tapestry was made in England there seems no reason to invent a prototype *chanson de geste* for it, for there is already a literary form consonant with the Tapestry within the tradition of English heroic poetry. It is interesting that there is no real condemnation of Harold in the Tapestry; he is portrayed, as we have seen, as a hero and meets an heroic death. The only criticism of him is the implied criticism of the sworn oath. He fits the heroic mould, whilst the English undertones occasionally detected in the hanging (some of which have been mentioned in the previous chapter) support an argument for an English literary form behind the Tapestry. It is further not without interest that the Tapestry presents a choice common in Germanic heroic literature, the choice between two courses of action, both of which are wrong but one of which is inevitable – in this case Harold's choice between breaking his oath or disobeying the instructions of the dying Edward. Though too much should not be made of this motif it might add strength to an argument against the *chanson* theory.

Dodwell, however, is surely right in suggesting a secular use for the Tapestry; it is irrelevant in this context whether the model was the *chanson de geste* or English heroic poetry. The Tapestry is on a domestic scale and its width would be lost against the height of the Romanesque cathedral of Bayeux. Its subject can be interpreted as secular or religious, but the action is the heroic action recounted at a feast in hall (feasts incidentally form an important element in the Tapestry). At no place is the Tapestry recorded as a relic; it is merely displayed on the feast of relics, presumably as an object of great venerability and considerable curiosity. It is more on the scale of the hall of a great magnate.[164] It would of course be lost within the great eleventh-century hall at Westminster, which measures *c*. 73 × 20.5 m,[165] but it would be comfortably housed within the twelfth-century building known as the Hall of the Exchequer inside the royal castle at Caen (30.7 × 11 m).[166] There would be no difficulty in finding a secular building in either England or Normandy which could house it.

I see the Bayeux Tapestry as the adornment of a secular hall – perhaps that of the warrior bishop Odo of Bayeux – based on a tradition, almost certainly English, of the heroic poem. I am not, however, willing to commit myself for or against the theory that the oath scene is central to the story.

Where was it made and when?

The inscription and the style of the Tapestry give some clues as to its origin. The inscription tells us that it is English. First, epigraphically, the crossed Ð (ð– with the value th) in the name Gyrth is apparently an English form. I discount the recently made suggestion that the cross-element in the Ð is a later addition simply because it does not appear in de

Fig. 2 Fragment of an English textile now in the Museo di
S. Ambrogio, Milan.

Montfaucon.[167] De Montfaucon would probably not have known about Anglo-Saxon scripts and Stothard, who first recorded it, would surely have questioned it if it had been doubtful; further examination by the 1983 conservators showed no evidence that the cross element was an addition. The abbreviation 7 for *et* (and) is another purely English form.[168] Other elements of the script are consistent with eleventh-century English forms. Elizabeth Okasha (who has kindly examined the inscription for me from an epigraphic point of view) has pointed to the difficulty of using comparative inscriptions in a discussion of the Tapestry as there are so few pieces with which to compare it – basically only the St Cuthbert embroideries noted above. It is, however, possible to say that the individual letters are drawn from a mixture of both epigraphic and manuscript models. Thus the form of the serifs of the letters is more typical of inscriptions, whilst the tall L and the word-dividing symbols are of a type more normally found in manuscripts. But the letter-forms themselves cannot date or localize the Tapestry, beyond indicating a strong likelihood that it was made in England.

Second, study of the language of the inscription has identified certain French elements, but more English ones. For example Michael Lapidge has pointed out to me that the verb *parabolare* (pl. 10) 'is the natural Latin form to be used by a speaker of French', being the direct source of the modern French *parler* (to speak). Although there are other French taints, such as CABALLUS, names and elements like CEASTRA, EADWARDUS and BAGIAS

are normally accepted as Old English rather than Norman forms.[169] The slip of Old English whereby Latin AD becomes Old English AT (pl. 49) may be the responsibility of an English scribe. Where there is a mixture of English and French (e.g. WILLELM) it is of a kind that might be expected in post-Conquest England.

Having suggested on the basis of the inscription that the Tapestry was made in England, can one support or strengthen the case or localize the place of manufacture more closely? Here we run up against the real difficulty of the unique nature of the Tapestry. There is no similar hanging in England. In scale it is different from other existing materials, from small manuscripts or from sculptural parallels. Although there are fragments of textiles on the Continent, particularly an English fragment in the Museo di S. Ambrogio in Milan (fig. 2), which can be loosely compared with the Bayeux hanging, their exact relations cannot easily be worked out. Closely parallel in technique and subject matter is a Norwegian textile fragment from Røn (fig. 3). Like the Bayeux Tapestry it is worked in laid and couched wool on a linen ground, with a similar outline stitch. To the left is a horse, separated from a number of prone (? dead) bodies by a tree. The bodies might be soldiers or clerics. There is a vegetal scroll border below this scene. The style of the foliage is of the twelfth century, perhaps late in the century. This fragmentary embroidery follows a tradition first encountered in Norway in the early ninth-century Oseberg ship burial,[170] a tradition which continues in Scandinavia until the fifteenth

Fig. 3 Fragment of a Norwegian hanging from Røn (Universitetets Oldsaksamling, Oslo).

century,[171] but which has little relevance here beyond showing that such hangings existed in northern Europe at this period. Save in Iceland, laid and couched work is not encountered in northern Europe after the twelfth century. The tradition is visible, but we have no idea of the spread of this particular technique outside England and Scandinavia. Such parallels are curiosities, hinting at the wealth of the various types of hangings known from literature,[172] but of no use to us in determining the age and origin of the Bayeux Tapestry. The tapestry fragment from Baldishol, Nes, Hedmark, Norway (fig. 4), part of a textile calendar, has a specious resemblance to the Bayeux Tapestry in that it portrays a mounted knight clad in a manner similar to that at Bayeux. This fragment is normally dated to the late twelfth or even thirteenth century[173] and is a true high-warped tapestry, not an embroidery. I see this as a late reflection of the embroidery tradition of Bayeux.

There being no satisfactory textile parallel, we must now turn to sculpture. This was often painted and might well have given the same impression as an embroidered hanging. A remarkable parallel to the Tapestry in sculpture was found during excavations at the site of the Old Minster at Winchester (fig. 5). The fragment is made from Box Ground oolite (from near Bath), its surviving height is 69.5 cm and it is broken on all sides. It was presumably discarded when the church was pulled down in 1093–4 to make room for the Romanesque cathedral. Part of two scenes survives. In one an armed man is walking to the left. His head, feet and hands are missing. To the right is a man, with raised hands bound together and lying on his back. A dog or wolf touches his head. The bodies of both the man and the dog are missing and the front of the man's face is damaged. Biddle[174] has suggested that the dog's tongue extends into the man's mouth: closer examination, however, shows that whilst this may have originally been so, the critical portion of the stone is damaged in this place. Biddle has identified the scene with a story of Sigmund in *Volsunga Saga* (a saga written down in the twelfth century in Scandinavia, but presumably widely current long before that), the important element of which is that Sigmund bites a wolf's tongue whilst lying bound. Biddle has suggested that the most likely period for such a carving would have been the reign of Knut the Great (1016–35). Knut was married in the church and it is argued that the Sigmund story was common to the royal houses of Denmark and England. The scene itself is iconographically unparalleled.

Fig. 4 Part of a Norwegian tapestry from Baldishol (Kunstindustrimuseet, Oslo).

Fig. 5 Fragment of sculpture from the Old Minster, Winchester
(Winchester Cathedral).

Before we consider the identity of the scene and the date of the sculpture, the features related to the Bayeux Tapestry should be examined. First, the scene on the Winchester fragment apparently comes from a frieze (and in a sense the Bayeux Tapestry is a frieze). Second, the dress and accoutrements of the man are very similar to those of the warriors on the Bayeux Tapestry – the mail-shirt with its trouser-like leg protection and short sleeves. The undershirt is represented as a series of stripes as on the Tapestry. The scabbard is of similar form and in the same position as those on the Tapestry (although it is tied with straps). There is no doubt that there is a striking concordance between the two. The sculptured fragment is, however, more finely detailed and, being carved from stone, is of course more solid and rounded.

The sculpture is said by Martin Biddle to be 'unfresh, slightly weathered', and that, together with the 'somewhat damaged condition of the present stone', is 'convincing evidence that the sculpture was not new when discarded but was derived from some existing scheme'.[175] George Zarnecki has cautiously suggested a post-Conquest date for the stone.[176] It is clear that it must be dated before 1094, but apart from this one definite statement all else is hypothesis. The strongest argument for it being pre-Conquest lies in the identification of the scene with the Sigmund scene in *Volsunga Saga* and the theory that this saga had a common meaning in Denmark and England in the reign of Knut. The second strongest argument is that the stone is worn. The strongest arguments for a post-Conquest date are, (a) the comparison with the art of the Bayeux Tapestry (made more than thirty-five years after the death of Knut), (b) George Zarnecki's opinion that the solid rounded forms with well-defined contours are Romanesque rather than Anglo-Saxon and (c) the fact that the stone is not painted. This latter point needs explanation: much, but not all, Anglo-Saxon sculpture was painted and the more one examines such sculpture, the more paint appears in the interstices of the carving. This stone was excavated and cleaned in the most meticulous fashion and, unlike much other sculpture of the period, has not been scrubbed and maltreated over the years; it is unlikely, therefore, that traces of colour would have been lost if they ever existed. I have examined this sculpture under very strong light and with magnification and have been unable to see any trace of paint. While this is by no means a conclusive argument, it could be suggested that the fragment was abandoned unfinished (perhaps due to damage) at some time not long before the building of the present cathedral at Winchester (it does not even look very weathered for an oolite). Biddle's argument that the scene had a meaning common to Denmark and England is weak: there is no evidence of any familiarity with the story of Sigmund in English art and literature of the eleventh century. I have said elsewhere that the argument in favour of Knut is thin, 'when we remember that Knut was intent on becoming a Christian king and would probably not want to advertise his pagan ancestry',[177] and this remains my opinion. In a way, the comparison with the Bayeux Tapestry is not completely convincing in detail, but it must be said that the general parallel is good and a Romanesque date for the piece has formidable backing.

That said, there is no other sculptural parallel to such a frieze in the eleventh century; indeed nothing in the nature of a coherent frieze survives in England until that on the west front of Lincoln Cathedral, probably dated to the 1140s. Bury St Edmunds seems to have had a major frieze, which was finished before 1142, but this no longer exists.[178]

We are left to find other parallels in manuscripts and these can only be of limited value as the coarse detail of the Tapestry is very different from the fine lines of Anglo-Norman penmanship. At this stage we must also consider the borders of the Tapestry, which have certain diagnostic features. All our comparisons with manuscripts are bound to be comparisons of detail, the stance of a bird or a figure, the folds of dress or the form of trees and foliage. First, some analysis of the motifs in the Tapestry is necessary. The human figures are varied in stance and detail. Usually they have long legs – sometimes slightly spindly. When they gesture their fingers are exaggeratedly long, as if to emphasize animated instruction. The shoulders are often slightly humped and every effort is made to show the face in profile, although a three-quarter face is not rare. While the faces are in no sense portraits, they are not stereotyped, as is clearly demonstrated by such a group of people as that depicted in a boat (pl. 40, left), where chin shapes change and in one case a face sprouts a beard. Where the men do not wear mail, the dress is often picked out in a fashion which suggests folds. There appears to be some attempt to differentiate English and Normans by providing the former with long thin moustaches (e.g. pl. 9) and giving the latter a strange haircut (e.g. pl. 11) which leaves them clean-shaven over the whole of the back of their heads, but neither treatment is universal. (It is not without interest that there is a remarkable consonance between the bare-necked Normans of the Tapestry and a condemnatory description of Danish shaven necks in a late Old English letter.)[179] Women occur rarely in the hanging. All are hooded and wear long dresses. Horses occur with great frequency, usually bridled and saddled. They are always represented in profile and in some scenes show spectacular tumbles (as in the crossing of the River Couesnon, pl. 19, and at the Battle of Hastings, pl. 66). In many respects the horses are the most competently designed and realistic figures on the hanging. Although to a certain extent stereotyped, variation of the leg position and the

Fig. 6 Detail from a calendar (British Library, MS Cotton Tiberius B.V, fol. 7).

overlapping of legs and heads create a great feeling of bustle and sometimes of speed. Other naturalistic animals include a pack-pony (pl. 46) and a rather jolly cow (pl. 45), which looks more like a drunken Evangelist symbol than a serious milk-producing creature. There are one or two sheep (pl. 45) and a number of hunting dogs (pls. 2, 8, etc.).

The borders are filled with mythological and ornamental creatures and various activities, some of which are portrayed naturalistically and include, for example, ploughing, sowing, harrowing, hunting birds with a sling (pls. 10–11), bear baiting (pl. 12), deer coursing (pls. 12–13), dressing wood (while naked!) (pl. 17) and, of course (in the scenes below the Battle of Hastings), fighting men, the dead, dying, brutally severed limbs, weapons and looters. Most such scenes occur in the lower border as do further naturalistic animals (pl. 6), even some eels and fish in the borders below the River Couesnon (pl. 19) and some unexplained scenes. Mythological scenes and creatures occur amongst them: a centaur (pl. 12), for example, and dragons and wyverns with wings, sometimes breathing fire (pl. 14), as well as a pair of rather unconvincing camels (pls. 14–15). The upper border is, generally speaking, less historiated, decorated with single or paired animals and birds. The lower one has the more varied subjects described above, some of which form a sequence of the fables of Aesop, beginning with the story of the fox and the raven with the cheese (pl. 4).[180]

There is in the borders a considerable amount of vegetal ornament, most of it of acanthus-like form, but some representing more elaborate trees. Trees are also seen in some quantity in the main field of the Tapestry: substantial, with solid trunks and inter-laced upward-curved branches. Amongst the vegetal ornament of the border, particularly towards the end of the Tapestry, are tendril-like plants which have much in common with the appearance of late Anglo-Saxon gold filigree.[181] The other motifs and objects illustrated in the hanging are mainly naturalistic or formulaic and, save for the dragon-heads on the ships, of minimal stylistic importance.

Most of the stylistic parallels to the Bayeux Tapestry are to be found in English manuscripts of the first half of the eleventh century. Wormald, for example, paralleled the Tapestry's trees with those in Ælfric's paraphrase of the Hexateuch (British Library, Cotton Claudius B. IV).[182] This parallel is, however, perhaps a little far-fetched as the manuscript trees (as distinct from the acanthus motifs) are much freer and more tendril-like. Perhaps it would be better to compare the Tapestry trees with those in the calendar of British Library, Cotton Tiberius B. V (fig. 6). But, as so often, because of differences of scale and material such parallels are only very general. One tree, for example (pl. 3), has an interlacing character entirely unknown in the Anglo-Saxon manuscripts and certainly very different from trees which appear after the Conquest (compare those, for example, in the Arundel Psalter).[183] Norman manuscript art provides us with few parallels: Kauffmann has pointed out that Norman manuscript originality lay in the development by scribes of initial letters ('long illustrative cycles are scarce')[184] and the vegetal elements of the Tapestry are not found in the manuscripts.

If the foliate ornament and the trees are of little stylistic use, the same is true of the purely ornamental animals and birds in the borders which unfortunately belong to a series with roots in tenth-

Fig. 7 Censer-cover from Canterbury (British Museum).

Fig. 8 Capital in the south transept of Ely Cathedral.

century Anglo-Saxon art and a long history thereafter. Comparison can be made, for example, with birds and animals on the Canterbury censer-cover (fig. 7), on an enamel from Brasenose College, Oxford,[185] and with those caught up in foliage or interlaced with other animals in manuscript initials.[186] Again comparisons can only be made in a very general manner with Anglo-Saxon and Norman manuscripts. The division of the borders into fields by means of oblique lines is also an Anglo-Saxon feature of some antiquity. It perhaps harks back to the ninth century or even earlier, when animals are frequently contorted into small sub-triangular fields, and is clearly seen on the late tenth-century Canterbury censer-cover (fig. 7) and its parallels.[187]

Lions in the upper border (pls. 48 and 49) have been paralleled by George Zarnecki with beasts on a capital in the south transept of Ely Cathedral (fig. 8), which may be dated *c.* 1090. Zarnecki has also drawn parallels between two other animals (pl. 18) and the lions on the similarly dated tympanum at Milborne Port, Somerset.[188] He also draws certain less convincing parallels with the foliate motifs in similar contexts. Such motifs are all part of the Anglo-Saxon heritage but are not of significance in localizing or dating the Tapestry. These sculptural and metalwork parallels to the birds and animals are, however, rather better than many of those drawn from manuscripts, where such creatures normally appear only in the scrolls of initial letters.[189]

It is to the manuscripts that we must turn for parallels to the narrative scenes. Apparently telling parallels have been drawn by Dodwell with the manuscript of the Old English Hexateuch (British Library, Claudius B. IV). Some are particularly relevant; such scenes, for example, as that of Abraham casting sling-stones at birds (fig. 9), which is closely paralleled in the scene in the border of pl. 11. The most startling common feature in this parallel is the sling-stone, which is in exactly the same position in each scene – a coincidence which might be formulaic, but which is certainly remarkable. Parallels have also been drawn to other scenes in the Hexateuch, particularly to that of a servant waiting at table (fig. 10), which has a specious similarity to the servant in the Tapestry waiting on the banqueters at Hastings (pl. 48). Other parallels are either so trivial as to be meaningless – the way an archer wears his quiver,[190] shrouded corpses,[191] the manner in which Noah uses a side-axe to smooth a plank[192] – or formulaic, as in the treatment of buildings or ships. The Old English Hexateuch is unusual in that it is perhaps the only English manuscript of the second quarter of the eleventh century which is profusely illustrated with scenes of daily life, and it would consequently be strange indeed if there were no parallels to those which occur in the Tapestry. Other parallels – the method of depicting horses, for example – are by no

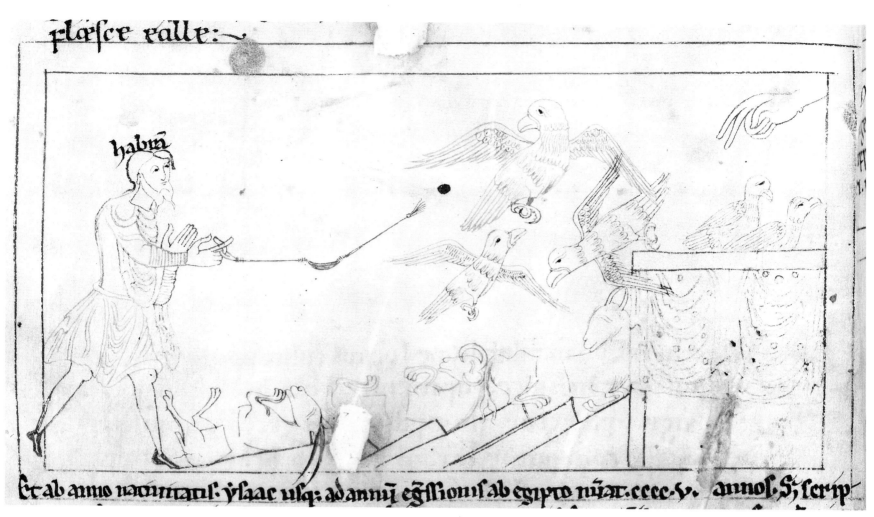

Fig. 9 Abraham casting sling-stones at birds (British Library, MS Cotton Claudius B.IV, fol. 26v).

Fig. 10 Servants waiting at table (British Library, MS Cotton Claudius B.IV, fol. 57v).

means so close. But ultimately comparisons are of little use in that the two cycles tell very different stories and have little stylistic consonance.

Other detailed comparisons have been picked out by Wormald,[193] most of which are merely interesting and undiagnostic. A ship's prow is a ship's prow is a ship's prow, whilst kings seated in the manner frequently seen in the Tapestry occur in English and Continental manuscripts and are based on the formulae of the late Carolingian and Ottonian manuscripts.[194] Much has been made of the humped-back figures which abound in the Tapestry. This feature, which was derived from Continental models in the tenth century, appears in English manuscripts throughout most of the eleventh century[195] and a similar trait is seen in contemporary Norman manuscripts,[196] which depended on English stylistic models.

One detail, however, might be of chronological significance. This is the treatment of certain tendrils which, as Wormald pointed out, are closely paralleled in the so-called 'Winchcombe' Psalter.[197] Wormald draws the parallel but does not follow it to a possible conclusion. The elongated tendrils in the border top left in pls. 1 and 6 are not dissimilar to the tendrils inspired by the Scandinavian Ringerike style which appear in the 'Winchcombe' Psalter and in the Old English Hexateuch.[198] Less clearly one might see a similar feature in the manes of at least two of the ships' figure-heads (pl. 6 left, prow, and pl. 42 centre, prow). The two manuscripts quoted as parallels date from the second quarter of the eleventh century and, although Ringerike details are found rarely in this country, they must, as Signe Horn Fuglesang suggested,[199] have had some effect on the English stylistic repertoire. Such elements do not appear in the Norman art of the same period, nor in English art of the post-Conquest period.[200]

The origin and date of the Tapestry

Where, then, was the Tapestry made? All the evidence adduced in this chapter points to an English origin. The story line, the heroic tradition and the artistic taste suggest this; the orthography of certain words makes it almost certain. It was presumably designed and executed by English artists and craftsmen. The subject might suggest that it was made for a Norman patron, but one must remember the parallel of Maldon, where it seems that a hanging commemorating an English defeat was presented to Ely by the defeated leader's widow. It is possible that the patron of the Tapestry was Odo, Bishop of Bayeux, who appears in a leading rôle in the hanging and in whose cathedral it eventually found a home. This must be common ground. But whether it was made in Canterbury, as suggested by numerous scholars in

recent years, is not so certain. Such a suggestion is best supported by the parallels with details in manuscripts like the Old English Hexateuch, which was written in Canterbury, but the best narrative parallel is provided by the Winchester frieze and it is not inherently unlikely that it could have been made in Winchester. Embroiderers at Winchester had a long tradition of royal patronage, as is evidenced by the stole and maniple of St Cuthbert which were certainly made for an English queen and a bishop of Winchester in the early tenth century. The manuscript parallels and the fact that Odo of Bayeux was earl of Kent and a patron of St Augustine's Abbey have persuaded scholars of the Canterbury origin. But Odo was never archbishop of Canterbury and if the Tapestry were made in Kent it is just as likely that it would have been made at one of his estates there, or in a nunnery under his patronage. But of this we know little. If it was made in Kent it might have been produced at the great nunnery at Minster-in-Sheppey; but Odo (who was a major landowner owning some 439 manors in seventeen southern and Midland counties at Domesday) would have spent much time at court, one of the chief centres of which was Winchester. If the Tapestry was produced there the most likely house for it to have been made in was the Nunnaminster (St Mary's). But need the Tapestry have been made by nuns, or even by women? The answer is, probably by women, but not necessarily by nuns. Documentation concerning embroiderers is scarce: Dodwell has listed and analysed the sources[201] and produced aristocratic, royal and ecclesiastical needlewomen who sometimes had women to help them in their task. There seems to be no mention of male needleworkers.

To summarize then, the Tapestry was certainly made in southern England, presumably by English designers and needlewomen; it was probably made for Odo and certainly acquired by him for his cathedral town.

How, then, is the Tapestry to be dated? Almost all the stylistic parallels are Anglo-Saxon, nothing is diagnostically post-Conquest. So little is known of the art of the immediately post-Conquest period that it would be difficult to place it in a period very soon after the events it portrays, were it not for the vegetal feature of the elongated tendrils just discussed. Such an element is not easy to find in England much after the middle of the eleventh century. Unless it was very old-fashioned when the Tapestry was designed, this motif might indicate a date near to 1066, say in the ten years after the Battle of Hastings. If it was made for Odo, it would have been made before his death in 1097 and almost certainly before 1082 when he was imprisoned by William.[202] Any later date seems improbable on stylistic grounds.

V Buildings, Dress and Objects

FOR MORE THAN a century the Bayeux Tapestry has been used as a quarry for illustrations of the warfare and daily life of early medieval people.[203] Rarely has it been used critically. The number and diversity of the subjects illustrated are enormous. According to Simone Bertrand the Tapestry portrays 626 people, 202 horses or mules, 55 dogs, 505 animals of all sorts, 37 fortresses or buildings and 41 ships or boats.[204] To these can be added innumerable categories of objects – weapons, clothes, table-ware, a plough, spades, a harrow and many objects and details which have provided illustrative fodder for the social and economic historian, for the archaeologist and for the historical journalist.

It is, however, important to examine this material critically, to ponder the sources and the likely models for the items portrayed. The Anglo-Saxon artist, so far as we know, did not go out into the countryside with a sketchbook in search of original objects or sites. Rather he would construct his pictures from memory, from imagination or from scenes – often Biblical – portrayed in books or paintings available to him. Thus it would be easy for him to draw a spade from memory, but more difficult to draw a representation of Westminster Abbey. In picturing Dol (pls. 20–21) he would have to use his imagination, basing his interpretation of it on the description of people who had been on the Breton campaign and presumably on any chronicle or history of these events which may have been available to him. Although some see the representation of Westminster Abbey (pl. 29) as at least a reliable indication of its general appearance, it must be noted that the representations of William's palace at Rouen (if indeed they are representations of the same building) are far from similar (pls. 16–17 and 34–35). If, however, the artist was using manuscript scenes as his model, they might not necessarily be the most reliable sources for contemporary forms. Manuscripts often have a prototype which is old or foreign. Consider for example the Harley Psalter (British Library, Harley 603), which was largely made at Canterbury in the middle of the eleventh century as a copy of the Utrecht Psalter (Utrecht University Library, Script. eccl. 484) which was made at Reims or Hautvillers in the first half of the ninth century and which was itself much influenced by the Eastern empire.[205] It is clear then that the objects and appearance of any building or person represented in the Harley Psalter cannot confidently be said to reflect the actual appearance of any

person or thing in eleventh-century England, for they could have been culled from Byzantine or Carolingian sources as much as two hundred years old.

This parallel is drawn only in a cautionary fashion; much of what appears in the Tapestry may well accurately reflect the actual appearance of things in England at the time of the Conquest. In some cases, however, the Tapestry may be misinterpreted, as for example in relation to the appearance of chain-mail trousers, which might well represent a split-skirted hauberk or a chain-trousered garment with a leather gore between the legs. Whatever our interpretation, it is clear that chain-mail had become depicted by a formula, repeated again and again in the Tapestry. A great deal of what is seen in the hanging is indeed formulaic and cannot be said to do more than indicate the object illustrated. A great deal more, however, is truly representative of the real thing. A definitive study of every detail represented on the Tapestry would be of considerable scholarly value, but within the scope of this study it seems more reasonable to group various related features together and pick out individual items for mention in the commentary to the plates (pp. 174–95).

Throughout this chapter it should be borne in mind that the Tapestry is unique. I have already emphasized that there is no existing contemporary delineation of historical events of the period, either in a manuscript or in embroidery. The Tapestry represents an immediate picture of eleventh-century secular events and it is for this reason that the historian and archaeologist use it as a quarry for the study of material culture. The only parallels of detail occur in religious and scientific books or in calendars which may – like the Harley Psalter – have elements derived from the other side of Europe. Furthermore, the archaeological record (though increasing year by year) is incomplete and can only occasionally illuminate the Bayeux Tapestry's presentation of objects and equipment.

Buildings

The structures most difficult of interpretation in the Bayeux Tapestry are the fortifications. Arguments concerning them have been endless, particularly in the last twenty years as the Tapestry has been used as a basis for a broad-ranging discussion concerning the origin of the private type of fortress of Norman origin based on a motte – essentially an artificial mound capped by a palisade or building. In order not to mis-

*Fig. 11 Capital from Westminster Hall showing a fortification on piles
(The Jewel House, Westminster).*

lead the reader in complicated argument I must state my conclusions before proceeding to a full discussion of the problem. I see the representations of most, if not all, the mottes in the Tapestry as the artist's convention for a fortification of any form. The motte might, therefore, represent a walled town, an encampment, a hill fort or any other major military work. I would argue that the artist – possibly a lay person of little military experience – had seen and been much struck by the large number of mottes built by the Normans after the Conquest. Such structures were new to England and to the artist, who understood this to be the normal Norman method of military fortification, not understanding that the Normans at home had ordinary town defences as well. If the artist was, as most commentators agree, an Englishman, he would not presumably have seen any of the fortresses he depicts in Normandy. To this man a fortification, *castellum, castrum, arx* or any of the many other words used to describe a Norman military work, was that typical Norman structure, a motte.

Although this is the case, I further believe that the representations of fortresses in the tapestry can be used by the historian of military engineering as evidence for the general structure and appearance of mottes in the late eleventh century. The artist knew what a motte looked like and knew how to draw it. What he could not draw in his linear style was the outwork or bailey which was normally constructed together with the motte, as without the use of true perspective it could not be rendered with any ease. For these reasons I first deny the Tapestry artist's representation of the fortresses as in any way indicative of the appearance of the actual sites or towns he is recording. I then discuss the fortresses depicted as representative of the general appearance of mottes; for the Tapestry provides, with one exception (a capital from Westminster, fig. 11), the only series of pictures – admittedly conventionalized – of Norman mottes of this very early period.

In the only case where the representation of a motte is actually mentioned in the inscription, at Hastings (pl. 49), the term CASTELLUM is used. It is

214

clear, however, as I have stated, that the artist interpreted most fortifications as mottes and that in only a few cases (as in pl. 13) did he make any real attempt to portray a different type of fortification – in this case probably a town wall with interval towers and a gateway (but see p. 216). It is always taken as axiomatic that the fortifications illustrated in the Tapestry at Dinan (pl. 23), Rennes (pls. 21–22), Dol (pl. 21) and Hastings (pls. 49–50) represent mottes with keeps (*donjons*) upon them,[206] although occasionally, as at Dinan, there has been some indecisiveness in the argument.[207] That there were mottes in Normandy before the Conquest is not in question,[208] but it should be emphasized that *sensu strictu* a motte is the base of a private fortification and not of a public protection of a town. This is not to say that a town could not have a motte, even if it was a private defensive work – indeed Richard I of Normandy is described as having *palatium sibi et arcem fabricans*[209] (built a palace and a castle), which, however we translate the word *arx*, implies a fortification in a town, a situation similar to that found in England immediately after the Conquest.[210] Three of the fortifications illustrated in the Tapestry are in Brittany (Dol, Rennes and Dinan). There is some hard evidence that mottes were being built in Brittany before 1066,[211] but none of these three places has yet produced the slightest trace of a motte at this date.

In England it has been argued that, if any mottes existed before the Conquest, they were built by Norman incomers – 'favourites' of Edward the Confessor – but it was not until the years immediately after the Conquest that mottes became a major feature of the feudal military control of the country.[212] It is, however, not certain that the pre-Conquest fortifications, usually described in Old English as *castel*, are necessarily mottes. The term is used for Dover, the ancient fortification of which can hardly be described as a motte, and it would be equally easy to translate *castel* as 'fortification' or even 'village'.[213] Further, the only excavations on an allegedly pre-Conquest motte, Richard's Castle, Herefordshire, have proved inconclusive.[214] The English were used to public fortifications. From the reign of Alfred onwards there had been a considerable programme throughout the length of the country. The products of this programme were town walls and palisades. Private fortification before the Conquest seems to have been confined to palisaded enclosures of the type excavated at Goltho, Lincolnshire.[215] To the English, however, the most notable feature of Norman fortification must have been the enormous number of mottes which were built by the Conqueror and his followers in the few years after the Conquest. I believe that this was the type of Norman fortification which most struck the designer of the Tapestry and that (whether public or private) they were all the same to him but worthy of variations of treatment.

If this is indeed so, it would then explain the most controversial representation of a military work on the hanging – the fortification at Hastings. This is described in the running text as CASTELLUM. It seems most unlikely that the first thing that William would do on landing in England would be to build a private fortification; rather as a good general he would surely build a temporary fortification or camp to protect his troops. Most commentators,[216] however, accept the former explanation, identifying the *castellum* of the Tapestry with the surviving motte at Hastings (which has provided no conclusive evidence of date).[217] It would seem reasonable to suggest that the designer of the Tapestry, having to conjure up an image for the word *castellum*, used his normal convention – a motte – to illustrate the invading army's earthwork.

Whilst the Tapestry represents mottes, the sites shown cannot be identified on the ground. We have noted that a motte survives at Hastings, but we need not identify this with the motte shown on the Tapestry. At Dinan there is no evidence of a motte, indeed this town is first mentioned in the Bayeux Tapestry; it is described as having walls of stone in the twelfth century.[218] Dol was also a town, the seat of an archbishopric, a considerable place; but we know of no motte there,[219] nor at Rennes, the capital of Brittany. In these cases it is clear that the mottes on the Tapestry represent fortified towns.

It is, nevertheless, worth examining the mottes in the Tapestry, for they give a good deal of information about eleventh-century fortification. Dinan and Dol (pls. 23 and 20–21) show a ditch with counterscarp round the base, whilst Rennes (pls. 21–22) appears to have a palisade and no ditch at the base. Steps are cut into the side of the mound at Rennes and appear to have been made of timber; they are consonant with the steps cut into the side of one of the two York mottes, Baile Hill, which were possibly wood-faced.[220] In three of the representations (pls. 20–23) a stepped bridge rises over the ditch to the top of the mound, in two cases apparently through gatehouses. The Dinan fortification (pl. 23) is clearly meant to be constructed of wood – soldiers are attempting to burn it – and, if the method of representing timbers is standard, it would seem that the fortification at Rennes (pl. 22) is also of timber, as are perhaps the breastworks below the dome at Bayeux (pl. 25). The fortifications at Dol, Rennes, and possibly Bayeux, are crenellated, whilst at Dol, Dinan and Rennes the keeps are apparently placed within an outer palisade. Brown has paralleled the layered effect of the representation of the mound at Hastings with the surviving remains at York, Norwich and Carisbrooke.[221] He has also pointed to the possibility that the timber tower at Dol (pl. 20–21) stood on posts in a manner seen on a capital from Westminster Hall (fig. 11)[222] and suggested archaeologically at Abinger, Surrey.[223]

Another type of fortification is to be seen in pl. 13 and Brown[224] has argued with some force that this is the tower of Rouen built by Duke Richard I in the late tenth century. It is portrayed as an ashlar building with corner turrets and crenellations, a prototype perhaps for the great keeps of the White Tower in London and Colchester. Although this is a convincing argument it might be safer to hedge the options, for it is equally possible to interpret this fortification as the walled town of Rouen itself,[225] a town known to the artist as William's Norman capital. The scene suggests, therefore, that William was meeting Harold outside the town as the latter was being escorted thither from his captivity with Guy of Ponthieu. A fortified town – Hastings – appears to be represented in pl. 51. This is, however, purely a conventional picture, and the scene is dominated by an immense iron-strapped door and a tower.

Palaces of royalty are depicted on the Tapestry in a number of places. They are all perhaps to be interpreted as an artist's convention in that they attempt to show both the inside and outside of a building at the same time, and that when the same building is depicted elsewhere there is no attempt at consistency. Perhaps the most interesting of these pictures is the representation of what must be William's palace at Rouen in pls. 16–17. This is apparently placed within a fortification, for it has a lookout tower to one side The full length of a ground-floor hall is shown; it has an arcade below the roof and a straight ridge-pole with floriated terminals and slanting gables. Two pillars indicate at the same time the walls and the method of supporting the roof. William sits at one end. This building is similar to what we know archaeologically of large halls from the Anglo-Saxon and Norman period. The arcading perhaps indicates a stone building. The clearest parallel is William Rufus's Westminster Hall, built in the 1090s, the largest hall of its kind in contemporary Europe.[226] Duke William's Rouen hall as shown in the Tapestry may have been similar to this, stone-built with an upper arcading, which at Westminster provided light, but which may equally at Rouen have been blind. The Anglo-Saxons were also familiar with large ground-floor halls; indeed at Cheddar a complete royal manor complex of the late tenth or early eleventh century has been excavated in which the main element is just such a hall, built not of stone but of timber.[227] This was replaced in the late eleventh century by a much grander timber hall. The remains of a major stone hall of the eighth or ninth century have been excavated at Northampton; this may have been a royal structure, but its foundations survive mainly as a robber-trench and add little to our knowledge of such structures save for its very early date.[228]

Every scene which depicts an English palace in the Tapestry is usually presumed to represent the old palace at Westminster.[229] If all the illustrations are indeed of one palace it is clear that they do not reflect English custom, for in the reign of William the Conqueror court was held at the three main feasts of the year in different places: in 1086, for example, the court assembled at Winchester at Easter, at Gloucester at Whitsun and at Westminster at Christmas,[230] and there is sufficient evidence in the Anglo-Saxon Chronicle and elsewhere to show that this followed an Anglo-Saxon tradition. Only in the scenes of Edward's death and of Harold after his coronation can we be sure that the events took place at Westminster – the other scenes could be anywhere. It is, however, highly likely that the palace shown in pl. 1 was at Winchester, for Harold sets out from seeing the king to ride to his estates in Bosham. This is only about 30 km distance; much closer than London. But the location is unimportant as the hall is highly conventionalized. The most informative scene is that which shows Edward's death (pl. 30) – a scene which suggests that it took place in an upper room or chamber, but the relationship of this to the great hall where Edward or Harold sit enthroned (pls. 1, 28, 31 and 32) is unclear. Brown[231] has pointed out that, if we can accept the upper chamber in pl. 30 as fact, the lower chamber was not being used for storage (a function normally attributed to ground floor accommodation of this sort). Most of the representations of the English palaces in the Tapestry appear to indicate, however, that the main accommodation consisted of a large hall with open timber roof, perhaps with a curved ridge-pole and roof lights and an opening to allow smoke to escape through a central turret (pls. 32–33). Angle turrets are normally represented on the exterior and an elaborate facade with central doorway is suggested in the first scene (pl. 1).

Two buildings of more than one storey are shown elsewhere on the Tapestry – one is Harold's hall at Bosham (pl. 3), with its outside staircase and vaulted ground floor. The other (pl. 50) has been identified by Brown as a town house, 'presumably in Hastings'.[232] I can see no evidence for this, nor for his argument that it is open to the street at ground-floor level. The lower arch in this scene is surely formulaic and analogous to the three arches seen under the first floor at Bosham, which nobody would see as anything but the representation of an interior. What is certainly shown in the lower part of this scene is the interior of the house. Holger Schmidt tells me that he thinks it might represent the interior of a single storey house, the upper portion of the picture representing the exterior of the house (it is very similar in form to the house in pls. 45 and 46) and a similar interpretation of Westminster Hall (pl. 30) would not, if one accepts his thesis, be altogether unthinkable.

Brown[233] also identifies the building (pl. 27) where Harold makes his landfall on his return to England as a two-storey town house with a balcony. While such an interpretation is possible, it might be suggested (in view of the lookout positioned on the balcony) that this is a tower, possibly even the gateway to a town.

First-floor halls are well known in England in the Norman period,[234] and are now, through archaeology, becoming known in Anglo-Saxon contexts – at Cheddar and possibly at Sulgrave,[235] for example. It is probable that they were becoming reasonably common in towns as tenement sites became more valuable, but two-storied houses are not much in evidence until the late twelfth century.[236] There is, however, a possibility that some of the late tenth-century houses with sunken floors found in the excavations at Coppergate, York,[237] may have had upper floors.

Among other non-religious structures which appear on the Tapestry are the three houses in pls. 45 and 46, which are usually described as humble, small peasant houses,[238] but which are more likely to be, like the representation of Mont St Michel (pl. 19), larger houses portrayed from a distance, adding depth to the picture. (Indeed this attempt at perspective occurs elsewhere in the Tapestry and is perhaps best seen in pls. 40–42 where small ships in the background are inserted to give an impression of the size of the large fleet.) One of these houses appears to be of stone, the other of log construction; one might have a thatched roof, two have shingled roofs and all have doorways in the middle of the long side. These seem to be conventions for reasonably substantial buildings and, merely because they are embroidered at a small scale, should not be taken to mean that they are peasant huts. There are two buildings on the Tapestry (pls. 11 and 37) which look more like bandstands than anything else. Sometimes known as *loges*, they have recently been more charmingly described as *kiosques*.[239] They have tegulated roofs and one has a cupola. These I take as representations of rather grand buildings, to be compared perhaps with the sketchy impression of Guy's hall in pl. 10. Similarly the rectangular frame around Ælfgyva (pl. 17) with its animal-head finials might also be seen as an artistic convention for a grand house. In the same scene is a tower (sometimes, in my view wrongly, interpreted as a dovecot), and other towers are placed at three or four places, as punctuation marks, throughout the Tapestry (pls. 16, 28, 50), representing gates, watch towers, *donjons*, churches or houses. Some buildings (e.g. pl. 47) are difficult to interpret coherently.

Three churches are shown in the Tapestry. Mont St Michel (pl. 19) is used as background: the well-known mount is clearly represented and a large arcaded structure is placed on a platform on top of it. Bosham has been much discussed. Fragments of an Anglo-Saxon church have survived at Bosham and attempts have been made to identify them with the Tapestry representation (pl. 3). Though one must

deny that the Tapestry is a 'suspect source'[240] in all matters, one might agree that any relationship between the surviving Anglo-Saxon parts of Bosham church and its representation in the Tapestry is purely coincidental.[241] Bosham church as shown in the Tapestry is simply an artist's convention for a building (the crosses at the gables and the inscription identifying it as a church); otherwise it is very similar in form to the simple houses discussed above (pls. 45 and 46), but produced on a larger scale. Brown points out that two churches are recorded at Bosham in Domesday Book and that it is more likely 'that the earl would visit the church pertaining to his manor rather than the collegiate establishment which is now the church at Bosham'.[242]

The representation of the great abbey church of St Peter at Westminster (pl. 29) must be taken more seriously. Westminster Abbey was refounded by Edward the Confessor, consecrated on 18 December 1065, and received the body of its patron a few days later.[243] A description of the church is given in some detail in the *Vita Ædwardi* and Richard Gem's translation of it is worth quoting:

And so, at the king's command the work, nobly begun, is being prepared successfully; and neither the outlay nor what is to be expended are weighed, so long as it proves worthy and acceptable to God and blessed Peter. The house of the principal altar, raised up with very high arches [or vaults], is surrounded with squared work and even jointing; moreover, the periphery of the building itself is enclosed on either side by a double arch of stones, strongly consolidated with a joining together of work from different directions. Further on is the crossing of the temple; which might surround the central quire of those singing to God, and with its twin abutment from different directions might support the lofty apex of the central tower; it rises simply, at first, with a low and strong vault [or arch]; grows, multiple in art, with very many ascending spiral stairs; then, indeed, reaches with a plain wall right up to the wooden roof, carefully roofed with lead: indeed, disposed below and above, lead out chapels, fit to be consecrated by means of their altars to the memories of the apostles, martyrs, confessors and virgins. Moreover, this multiplicity of so vast a work is set out so great a space from the East [end] of the old temple that, of course, in the meantime the brethren staying therein might not cease from the service of Christ; and furthermore so that some part of the nave to be placed between might advance.[244]

There is, as Gem points out, a general accord between this description, the depiction of the church in the Tapestry, and

to some extent . . . what is known from other sources. Details to be noted are the presbytery of two bays; the crossing tower with flanking turrets, and with secondary turrets (possibly at the ends of the transepts); and the arcaded nave of five bays (with eight bays of windows). The last seems to show clearly shafts rising up the walls over the piers; but this feature also occurs elsewhere in the tapestry in a probably wooden structure at Bosham, and another at the scene of the preparations in Normandy for Duke William's invasion. It has been suggested that the absence of any western towers in the tapestry indicates that these features were not completed by the time of its execution and this may be so. Most of the information derived from the tapestry, however, is merely confirmation of what is known from other sources; and any details which cannot be verified should be treated with reserve.[245]

This seems to be as definitive a statement concerning the representation of Westminster Abbey on the Tapestry as one is likely to achieve, and the last sentence should be taken as text by all students of the Tapestry as a whole.

Furniture and fittings.

The Bayeux Tapestry is a splendid source for an understanding of the material culture of the eleventh century. Not least interesting in this respect are the furnishings of houses and churches. Again, it must be pointed out that some of these representations are formulaic: some of the seats, for example, are certainly thrones rendered in a manner common since the Carolingian period,[246] whilst the reliquaries on which Harold swears his oath (pls. 25–26) can hardly be regarded as accurate renderings of the actual shrines available at Bayeux. But many scenes give an insight into daily life at all levels and sometimes considerably illuminate our view of the period.

As an example, an examination of the scene of Edward's death and enshroudment (pl. 30) reveals both problems and points of interest, incidental intelligence and matters of curiosity. Edward is shown dying in bed supported on a pillow by a servant, with an unshaven cleric blessing him. Harold is probably the figure in the foreground and the woman to the far left is probably Queen Edith – Harold's sister. Below, as though on the ground floor of the house, Edward is being placed in his shroud in the presence of a cleric. The bed in which Edward is dying is curtained and hangings like this may be seen elsewhere in English drawings;[247] I know of only one English find of such textiles (identified as 'hangings'), in the seventh-century royal burial at Sutton Hoo.[248] The pillow – together with the cushions which appear in many scenes (e.g. pl. 1) – is a type of object relatively common in early medieval Europe, but known in England only at Sutton Hoo.[249] The pillow is rather large and might be described by the modern word 'bolster', as may a similar pillow, for example, in a Nativity scene in a manuscript painted under English influence at St Bertin in the late tenth century (Boulogne, Bibiliothèque Municipale, MS 11).[250] In one Old English source it is stated that a bolster (*bolster*) is for the neck and a cushion (*pyle*) is for the arms;

Fig. 12 The 'great bed' from Oseberg, Norway (Universitetets Oldsaksamling, Oslo).

the former is therefore a most appropriate word for the object in pl. 30.[251] Other bolsters and cushions are illustrated in Anglo-Saxon manuscripts[252] and it is clear that these objects were familiar to both Anglo-Saxons and Normans. The Tapestry thus provides confirmation of a fact known from other sources. Beds, because of the frequency of the portrayal of the Nativity, are encountered fairly often in Anglo-Saxon manuscripts.[253] Although traces of beds have not been found in English excavations after the pagan Anglo-Saxon period, the late ninth-century burial from Oseberg, Norway, produced three complete beds,[254] one of which ('the great bed', fig. 12) has animal-head posts at the head not unrelated to that which appears at the foot of Edward's bed in the Tapestry. A bed with an animal-head post is also seen (looped by a curtain) in the Old English Hexateuch.[255]

Sometimes the information provided is simply a matter of curiosity. For example, the scene where Edward is wrapped in his shroud (pl. 30) is a commonplace. Such scenes are formulaic in manuscripts,[256] but Dodwell has pointed out that fragments of Edward the Confessor's shroud (or at least silk removed from his tomb in 1685 or 1686) survive and are preserved in the Victoria and Albert Museum.[257] Whether these are from the first entombment of the body or not, it is at least a curious and interesting fact.[258]

This example of the analysis of a single scene in the Tapestry demonstrates its richness as a source for the understanding of the general accoutrements of daily life in eleventh-century England. In a study of this length it is impossible to do justice to the whole range of detail shown in the hanging. In some instances we are given a unique insight into life in that period and, while bearing in mind the conventionalization, we should not forget that real life is breathed into the story. Eating at table is a day-to-day occurrence which is represented in manuscript illumination throughout the eleventh century. Often it is an expression of a formula (the Last Supper, for example) and Dodwell in particular has shown parallels for the stance of waiters and the disposition of people between pl. 48 of the Tapestry and the Old English Hexateuch.[259] In no other source, however, are we provided with scenes of *alfresco* preparation of food (pls. 46 and 47), with a cauldron suspended from a bar over a brazier, with something that looks very much like a portable oven, with a temporary table of shields, a strange cooking fork and spitted meat and fowl. Nowhere else do we see the blessing of food at a secular meal or the summoning of guests to table by a blast on a horn. These unconscious, almost impromptu, touches are perhaps the most instantly striking elements in the Tapestry and convey the temper of daily life more impressively than many manuscript set-pieces – even those chief quarries for researchers into Anglo-Saxon daily life, the calendars. It is for this reason that scholars turn again and again to the Tapestry for visual confirmation of facts of daily life at the upper end of society.

The material culture of this period surviving in the archaeological record provides illumination of many scenes in the Tapestry. English sources are thin and Norman sources practically non-existent, but in what follows I have first tried to find parallels in English sources (sometimes quite old ones), but have frequently had to turn to Scandinavia for parallels partly because the survival of the pagan practice of burial with grave goods continued much longer there than in England or Normandy. But the Scandinavian parallels are also valid in another fashion: both England and Normandy had Scandinavian roots. William's family and those of some of his chief followers came from Scandinavia and he had Scandinavian relatives. England had been ruled by Scandinavian kings until 1042 and was run in tandem with Denmark for more than twenty years up to that date. The cultural traits of all three countries clearly affected each other.

Clothes, arms, armour and regalia
The dress of the people represented in the Tapestry is fairly standardized and clearly related to that which appears in the manuscript and sculptural tradition of the tenth and eleventh centuries. No major article of clothing in any way comparable to that which appears on the Tapestry – other than shoes, which are of fairly basic form[260] – survives physically from this period. Apart from the ankle-length tunics (e.g. pl. 48) which are worn by important people when sitting down, two forms of male dress are seen – a knee-length tunic and a rather full-legged, trousered garment which stretches below the knee where the legs are normally trimmed with braid (e.g. pls. 10–11). At the neck of both garments is a slit, usually shown with a braided border. The tunic occasionally has a braided hem (pl. 6) and in one case appears to have a fringed hem (the man behind the pillar in pl. 10). Long hose are normally worn, sometimes of banded pattern; some Normans (including William) are occasionally cross-gartered (pls. 15–17). In pl. 13 William wears garters below the knee which have braided ends hanging almost to the ankle; in pl. 16 the cross-gartering has a single pendant strap-end. The dwarf-like figure in pl. 11 apparently wears long trousers underneath what is either a split-skirted tunic or longish over-trousers (cf. also the late twelfth-century Baldishol tapestry, fig. 4). In one of the representations of Guy (pl. 10) the tunic is clearly patterned and, in this case at least, not belted – Nevinson has suggested that it is a military cloak or tunic, a wambase or gambeson, or a decorative version of the 'gipoun, which was generally worn under mail'.[261] A similar but trousered garment is worn by a

rider (could it be Guy?) in pls. 18–19 and once again by Bishop Odo in pl. 67. Generally it would seem that tunics are worn by the higher orders: servants and messengers generally wear trousers (cf. pls. 10, 11, 47). But this is by no means universally true, as the shipwrights, for example, apparently wear tunics (pl. 36) and William's messenger, a man of some importance, is shown in trousers in pl. 11. In a number of cases the tunics are tied at the waist to leave bare legs, either for convenience during work (pl. 36) or for wading in water (e.g. pls. 4, 6, 37).

In no case is any form of civil head gear worn by a man. A cloak is frequently depicted fastened on the right shoulder to leave the right arm free. When seated or seen in profile (pl. 2) it falls in folds in front and hangs below tunic length at the back (pl. 28), but when standing with the body towards the viewer the cloak is worn with the fastening at the centre of the neck and is allowed to fall off both shoulders (pl. 31). The more important men sometimes fasten their cloak with a disc brooch (pl. 2) of a type well-known in the late Anglo-Saxon period: such brooches are usually made of silver, but at least one example inlaid with gold is known.[262] Edward (pl. 28), Harold (pl. 31) and William (pl. 10) wear a rectangular brooch, but no other form of male jewellery is shown in the Tapestry. In pl. 14 William is shown with a rather more square-cut, hip-length cloak with two ribbons at the neck.

The cleric in the enigmatic Ælfgyva scene (pl. 17), who is distinguished by a tonsure, wears dress of purely secular form (his cloak is clasped at the neck). The same is true of Odo, as seen just before Hastings with William and his brother Robert, save that his tunic seems to be slightly longer than those of his brothers (pl. 48). Some of the men following the bier of Edward the Confessor (pl. 30) are distinguished as priests by their tonsure and in one case by a crozier, but are otherwise represented in lay clothes. The bishops in the scenes concerned with the death and burial of Edward and the coronation of Harold (pls. 30 and 31) wear liturgical dress – a chasuble with a long orphrey for the cleric present at Edward's death, whilst Stigand at Harold's enthronement wears a chasuble and carries a maniple in his left hand. His stole appears above his alb. The highly decorated stole and maniple of superb craftsmanship associated with the shrine of St Cuthbert in Durham Cathedral are the only remaining vestments of their type from the Anglo-Saxon period; they were made in Winchester and were probably presented by King Athelstan about 934.[263]

Only three clothed women are portrayed in the Tapestry (pls. 17, 30 and 50). All have a covered head – an uncovered head was improper in a woman.[264] They wear voluminous dresses which, in the two cases where they can be seen, sweep the ground and have long sleeves. They all wear a kerchief or hood, which in the case of the woman figured in pl. 50 is tucked into the round neck of her gown. In this case also the sleeve of an undergarment protrudes at the left cuff. In the scene of the death of Edward (pl. 30), the sleeve of the woman's undergarment can be seen as she lifts her kerchief to her eyes. In no case are women represented wearing jewellery.

The arms and armour of the soldiers in the Tapestry have been much studied, particularly in the masterly survey of Sir James Mann.[265] Here I can only summarize much of his work and add a few notes which will bring it more up to date. Seventy-nine men wearing body armour appear in the Tapestry; as well as this we have representations of arms being carried to the ships (pl. 38). This is far beyond the number of armed men appearing in any Anglo-Saxon or Norman pictorial source. The Tapestry also seems to distinguish between the professionally mounted and armed warrior and the defensive levy, the English *fyrd*, which was without armour and ill-equipped. But this distinction only occurs consistently in the last surviving scene (pl. 73) and in the scene where the Normans attack the English on the hill (pl. 66). Otherwise both English and Normans seem similarly accoutred.

It is easy to make too much of the difference between Norman and English armour. The upper ranks of English society in the early eleventh century had to pay on the death of every man of thegnly rank a *heregeata* (a payment of war-gear), comprising horse and weapons. This in the reign of Knut consisted of a helmet, mail-shirt, sword, spear and shield, together with one accoutred horse.[266] It is no surprise then to see English and Norman soldiers in the Bayeux Tapestry armed in the same fashion. At the time of the Battle of Hastings the feudal obligation encompassed in the description 'knight' had no meaning in England – although it pertained in Normandy. I, therefore, use this term sparingly, and specifically in relation to the Normans.

The principal defensive armour portrayed on the Tapestry consists of a long mail-shirt, a conical helmet with nose-guard and a kite-shaped shield (although a few circular shields are represented). The leaders occasionally wear mail leggings and two of the archers wear pointed hats, presumably of leather (pl. 60). The arms of offence are sword, mace or club, axe, spear, lance and bow and arrows.

The mail-shirt is the most impressive piece of armour pictured in the Tapestry: obviously heavy and valuable, it is seen carried between two men on a pole in pl. 38. The chainwork itself is represented conventionally in a number of ways; as rings, as squares and as lozenges, but there can be little doubt that this is indeed chain-mail composed of interlinked metal rings. The mail-shirt apparently had trouser-like legs which reached to the knees, where they were bound with another material. In many cases they are depicted with a square panel on the chest (e.g. pl. 38), a feature never satisfactorily explained, but which is paralleled in an eleventh-century Spanish manuscript.[267]

Chain-mail shirts are known from the Late Roman Iron Age onwards in northern Europe.[268] None are known from Normandy and only one mail coat has been found in an Anglo-Saxon context, that from Sutton Hoo, Suffolk, which is so rusted together that its original form can no longer be interpreted. It is 'made of alternate rows of welded or forged links and of riveted links'.[269] Only a single other find of Anglo-Saxon mail exists. This is the neck-guard of an eighth-century helmet from Coppergate, York (fig. 13),[270] which is of exactly the same type of interlocking rings as the mail from Sutton Hoo. A rare Anglo-Saxon picture of a man wearing a mail-shirt occurs on the eighth-century Franks' Casket.[271] Mail-shirts are not often depicted in English manuscripts before the twelfth century, but the early eleventh-century depiction of a king in chain-mail in the Old English Hexateuch representation of the battle against Sodom and Gomorrah[272] is very similar to the form of the mail in the Tapestry, except that it is not bound at the knee and could therefore represent a tunic with a split skirt (fig. 14). After the Conquest (and particularly in the twelfth century), representations of warriors wearing chain-mail become more common, both in manuscript and in sculpture.[273]

I have deliberately avoided calling this garment a *hauberk* or *byrnie* as it appears to have been more than the simple mail-shirt or tunic seen, for example, in late eleventh-century French manuscripts.[274] It can hardly have been possible, even for the hardiest Norman, however well-padded, to wear chain-mail between his legs when sitting astride a horse. Is it possible that, if the garment was indeed constructed in the manner shown in the Tapestry, the poor men had a gusset of leather rather than chain between their thighs? The only physical evidence to the contrary comes from Russia, where an undated pair of chain-mail trousers was recorded in the Scheremetev collection at the end of the last century.[275] It is to my knowledge unique and, if genuine, is probably late and far from the tradition known in the medieval west. However, some of the foot soldiers in the Tapestry are shown with fully mailed trousers (pl. 64). Brooks and Walker[276] have taken these latter scenes and compared them with the Winchester sculpture (fig. 5). They have suggested that trousered mail was an English fashion used by foot soldiers. Their argument is reasonable, but I would maintain against it that the trousers would still be uncomfortable, and that the artist – although well informed – must not always be taken too literally. An argument against taking such depictions literally is provided by a number of scenes (e.g. pl. 24) where the sword is apparently worn down the trouser leg,

Fig. 13 Helmet from Coppergate, York (York, Castle Museum).

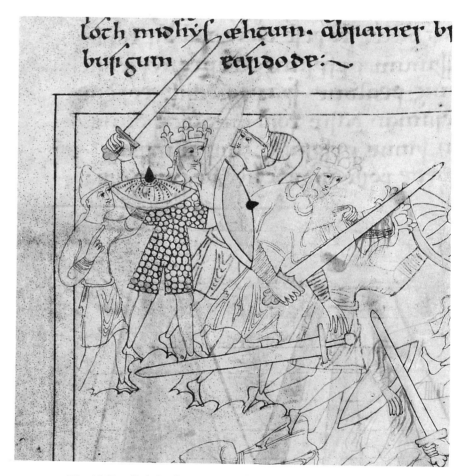

Fig. 14 Detail of a battle-scene (British Library, MS Cotton Claudius B.IV, fol. 24v).

the hilt and tip of the scabbard being clearly represented. Even if the trousers were knee-length, walking with such a cumbersome article so close to the thigh would be both uncomfortable and impractical. Finally, as I still feel doubtful concerning the form of the mail garment in the Tapestry, it is worth looking at the examples in pls. 37 and 38 where, stretched on poles, they look less convincing as trousered garments; more like a split-skirted hauberk.

Mail leggings, which are worn only by the most senior Normans on the Tapestry (e.g. pl. 54), certainly existed and are paralleled for instance on the effigy on the tomb of one of William's sons, Robert, Duke of Normandy, in Gloucester Cathedral (fig. 15).

As a footnote to the discussion of chain-mail it is worth noticing that occasionally a mailed hood (e.g. pl. 55) is represented: in many other cases (e.g. pl. 57) mail appears to rise from the mail-shirt to disappear under the helmet, indeed in most cases the neck seems to be protected by mail – one is reminded here of the mail neck-guard on the York helmet (fig. 13). The continuation of the mail-shirt under the helmet is exactly paralleled in an early twelfth-century French manuscript,[277] and in the Baldishol Tapestry (fig. 3), but the way in which this functioned has never been satisfactorily explained.

The second article of defence portrayed in the Tapestry is the helmet. It normally consists of a simple, slightly pointed cap with a nose-guard apparently constructed of a number of small plates or strips of metal, and is occasionally depicted with a neck-guard (pls. 24 and 38). It bears no resemblance to the two earliest Anglo-Saxon helmets, from Benty Grange, Derbyshire,[278] and from Sutton Hoo,[279] although a neck-guard not unlike that which occurs on the Sutton Hoo helmet is represented on the Tapestry (cf. pl. 38). Although nose-guards appear on late Roman helmets,[280] the idea of a nose-guard is so obvious that such parallels are mere curiosities. The only other surviving helmet from Anglo-Saxon England is that from Coppergate, York, which is probably three hundred years older than the Tapestry (fig. 13). This helmet has a nose-guard but it is a very slight affair – purely ornamental – indeed, the helmet itself must be seen as a direct descendant of the Roman parade-helmet and its derivatives like that from Sutton Hoo.

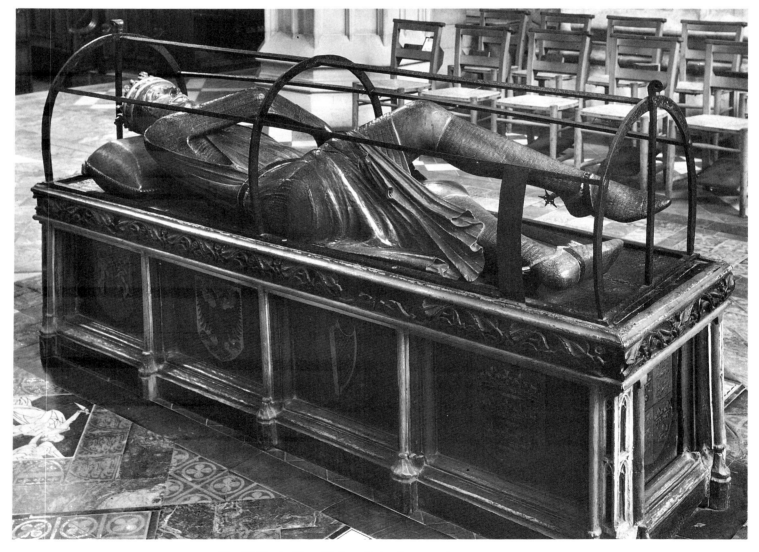

Fig. 15 Tomb effigy of Robert, Duke of Normandy, early 13th century
(Gloucester Cathedral).

Fig. 16 'Helmet of St Wenceslas' (Treasury of Prague Castle).

century in Continental manuscripts, as for example in the Golden Gospels of Echternach (fig. 17).[289] Although the kite-shaped shield is found in the hands of both the English and the Normans, there is some attempt by the artist of the Tapestry to distinguish the circular Anglo-Saxon shield (pl. 64) from the kite-shaped shield of the Normans, and it may well be that the latter was introduced from the Continent at about the time of the Conquest. It was a new fashion and was essentially a cavalry weapon; it covered the leg as well as the body. No such shield survives and, like other medieval shields, it was presumably made of perishable material like wood and leather. The Tapestry clearly shows the method of holding the shield on the left arm through a loop on the back of the shield, the hand grasping another loop (e.g. pl. 69). When not in use the shield was slung over the left shoulder so that both hands could be left free for the reins (pl. 44): a shield with this sling is seen, for example, amongst the debris of battle in the border of pl. 64, or in great detail in pl. 20. There was no central boss, as on the round Anglo-Saxon shield (where it was functional in that it protected the hand), but there is some indication on the Tapestry that a decorative boss was placed in the centre to make a pattern with the heads of the rivets which held the straps on the back. As has frequently been pointed out, some of the kite-shaped shields in the Tapestry are decorated with motifs which look like heraldic devices (particularly pl. 70). We have no evidence of formal heraldry at this early stage of feudal society, but personal marks of difference may already have been placed on shields.

The circular shield of traditional Germanic form with central pointed iron boss and bound rim appears occasionally in the hands of Anglo-Saxon

A particularly important parallel to the Bayeux Tapestry helmet is the so-called helmet of St Wenceslas now in the Treasury of Prague Castle (fig. 16).[281] The decoration of the nose-guard is clearly of tenth- or eleventh-century date and the helmet was certainly made in northern Europe. The pointed cap is made of a single sheet of iron with an applied nose-guard and lower rim. Another parallel is provided by a plain helmet, made from a single piece of metal with rivet holes at the rim for a neck-guard, which comes from Olomouc in Moravia;[282] it is undecorated and therefore cannot be dated. The lines seen on the caps of many helmets in the Tapestry (e.g. pl. 24) might represent bands, as on the helmet from Chamoson, Switzerland,[283] which is perhaps similar to those in pl. 24, or more probably may indicate panels of iron plate like that on the helmet found in a tenth-century grave in Russia, at Gnezdovo, near Smolensk.[284] (Scandinavian burials occur in this cemetery and the sword found with the helmet[285] would be quite acceptable in a Viking context.) Helmets of the Viking Age in northern Europe are extremely rare – two fragments from Gotland, one fragmentary helmet from Gjermundbu in Norway, and a fragment from Tjele in Denmark[286] are all that survive. Pictures are more common; Knut, for example, on coins issued in Winchester between 1023 and 1029, wears a conical helmet with nose-guard.[287]

The Tapestry is the first English source to show the kite-shaped shields which were to become so popular throughout western Europe in the course of the eleventh and twelfth centuries,[288] but which are illustrated as early as the second quarter of the eleventh

Fig. 17 Detail from the Golden Gospels of Echternach, fol. 78 (Germanisches Nationalmuseum, Nuremberg).

Fig. 18 Sword from Canwick Common, Lincoln (British Museum).

foot-soldiers on the Tapestry (pl. 64) or amongst the discarded arms in the border (pl. 70). Circular shields of the type shown on the Tapestry are familiar in Anglo-Saxon manuscripts of the period,[290] and have a long tradition which goes back to the pagan period. Shields of this form, represented by iron shield-bosses and grips, are frequently found in pagan graves.[291] The board, we know from literary sources and surviving fragments, was usually of lime-wood, the most complete reconstruction being possible at Sutton Hoo, although this is hardly typical.[292] Pictures of shields are rare before the early eleventh century, but good examples are provided on the eighth-century Franks' Casket, where circular shields are shown, held by a hand within a central boss.[293] The large circular shield was well-known on the Continent and is seen in manuscript illumination until the eleventh century.[294]

It may be assumed that the kite-shaped shield came in to replace the circular Germanic shield of the foot-soldier as a cavalry weapon in the early eleventh century. The Bayeux Tapestry (particularly in pl. 64) seems to reflect an actual change in military fashion. Circular shields continued in use well beyond the eleventh century, ending up as the Scottish targe in the eighteenth century, but later they were generally much smaller than the large early medieval shields which could be as much as a metre in diameter.

The most prestigious weapon of offence was the sword, although this was primarily used by warriors from the upper levels of society – a fact reflected in the Tapestry where by no means all the soldiers carry swords. Indeed, in pl. 61 it appears that only the leaders of the army carried swords, the majority being armed with spears or lances. The sword is slung from a belt (pl. 56) in a scabbard, perhaps best seen in pl. 69; details of the belts – buckles and strap-ends – are clearly shown in pl. 9. The sword is of a type well-known from finds and manuscript illumination of the period. Held in one hand, it has a broad, straight blade with parallel edges, is a little over 90 cm long and has a straight guard with a simple rounded or lobed pommel. It was a slashing, not a thrusting, weapon. The Tapestry shows a number of swords with guards curved towards the grip (pl. 69), a form not encountered among surviving swords. English guards curved away from the grip are well

known (fig. 18),[295] and the fact that the artist has apparently reversed the guard may be another example of his lack of military knowledge. Swords with straight guard and D-shaped pommel (as in the centre of the lower border in pl. 64) are found throughout Europe from the ninth century onwards.[296]

Figs. 64 and 65 demonstrate that sword and lance were not exclusive weapons, but it is clear from the Tapestry that the lance or spear was not only the commonest, but also the most normal, weapon of the foot soldier. Those illustrated in the Tapestry are insubstantial, often represented merely by a line of stitches. They normally appear to be under two metres in length and have a head which is often represented in a different colour. Iron spearheads are commonly found in pagan Germanic graves,[297] but in later periods they are sometimes difficult to date, although they can occasionally be identified in the eleventh century by their ornament.[298] Various types of spearhead are depicted in the Tapestry but they are chiefly either barbed (pl. 56) or leaf-shaped (pl. 66). Examples of barbed spearheads of this period have not been identified, but leaf-shaped examples are common, varying in size, shape and length. Two short lines, often drawn below the spearhead, may represent nails or bars which often protrude on either side of the socket of a spear;[299] perhaps less plausibly this feature could represent the wings of a heavy hunting spear.[300] Spears are used in different ways; the mounted men use them either overarm (pl. 63) or couched in a manner which was to become much more familiar in the cavalry warfare of the Middle Ages, locked under the soldier's arm (pl. 64),[301] a position presumably also intended to be shown in the Baldishol tapestry (fig. 3). The cavalry have heavy saddles which would enable them to take the shock of lancing an opponent at speed. The foot-soldiers in the Tapestry all hold their spears overarm.

Some spears were also used as throwing weapons. Brown has pointed out that only one spear is seen in the Tapestry thrown from the Norman side (pl. 61) at the Battle of Hastings, whilst admitting that the Normans threw them at Dinan (pl. 23).[302] It would, therefore, be wrong to assume on the basis of the Tapestry alone that the Norman cavalry did not throw spears: the Tapestry should not be taken too literally and it might be safer to accept that at this time spears were used both as casting weapons and as hand-held weapons. It may be, however, that there was a distinction between the two types of spear – a distinction not recognized or portrayed by the Tapestry designer. Some spears carry small rectangular, curved or triangular banners (gonfanons) below the head (e.g. pl. 53); this is their first appearance in a secular context in Anglo-Saxon or Norman sources.

Archers appear on both sides in the Battle of Hastings, and are in one place portrayed as a massed body in the lower border of the Tapestry (pls. 68–69). Only one archer wears mail (pl. 60), otherwise they are dressed in normal clothes, perhaps padded (pl. 60, archer top left), and at least two of the archers wear leather Phrygian caps. All the archers carry quivers slung on their shoulders, but in one case the archer carries a bundle of arrows in his left hand with his quiver held at his belt (pl. 60). The fact that only one English archer appears in the Tapestry (pl. 60) must be taken as artistic licence; the English were familiar with the bow as a weapon in both literary and pictorial sources, as witness, for example, the poem *The Battle of Maldon*[303] and the Franks' Casket.[304] The bow was also, of course, extremely important as a hunting weapon.

Arrows were tipped with iron and flighted with feathers which are particularly well represented on the arrows in the shield of one of the foot soldiers in pl. 70. Many types of arrow-head are known in northern Europe,[305] but the barbed arrow-heads of the type shown on the Tapestry are practically unknown at this period,[306] although the Old Norse word *krókr* (a barb) probably implies the existence of such objects. That simple iron arrow-tips of other forms were also used in battle is suggested, for example, by those found in the tenth-century warrior's grave from the Ile de Groix in Brittany and elsewhere.[307] As the arrow-heads in the Tapestry are represented merely by two stitches it would be unwise to take their form too literally.

Only one roughly contemporary bow is known from northern Europe: possibly of tenth-century date, it comes from Hedeby in Schleswig-Holstein.[308] It is about 6ft long (192 cm) and is made of yew. This is different from other bows found in northern Europe,[309] and, although longer, is not unlike those used by the archers in the Tapestry.

Long-handled ceremonial axes appear occasionally in the Tapestry in the hands of the more important people – Guy of Ponthieu, for example (pl. 10). His axe appears to be about 1.5 m long and has a broad expanding blade. Other battle-axes occur in the Tapestry; Harold's brothers or their entourages fight with them at Hastings (pl. 64), and in pl. 65 an axe-head has been severed from its shaft by the blow of a sword. Axes had long been used in battle. In England battle-axes are featured on the Lindisfarne Stone[310] and are traditionally supposed to have been the chief

offensive weapon of the immediate entourage of the Scandinavian kings of England. In the Tapestry, although the axe is seen in non-English hands as a ceremonial weapon (pl. 10), it is depicted only as the weapon of an English foot-soldier at the Battle of Hastings (pls. 62, 64, 65, 70, 72). Whether the axe being carried by the Norman commissariat in pl. 38 is a weapon or a tool is open to question; if, as is possible, it is a weapon, this is the only indication of its use as a battle-axe by the Normans. The only complete hafted battle-axe known to me anything like those shown in the Tapestry is one which might be of twelfth-century date from Vorma, Eidsvoll, Akershus, Norway,[311] which is about 111 cm long. Axe-blades of the form found on the Tapestry are reasonably common (e.g. fig. 19).

The last group of weapons of offence to be considered are the maces and clubs. First let us dismiss the *baculum* held by Bishop Odo (pl. 67), which has been described as a mace. Allen Brown has denied this, writing that it is rather 'the eleventh-century equivalent of a field marshal's baton'.[312] While I would not draw this parallel I agree with the sentiment and have translated it as 'wand' – although it is a pretty heavy one. Michael Lapidge has pointed out to me that *baculum* in an ecclesiastical context is the normal word for a bishop's crozier in the early medieval period – perhaps 'wand of office' might be a better translation here. Maces or clubs are carried by the fleeing English *fyrd* (the levied army) in pl. 73 and another club is seen flying through the air in the heat of battle in pl. 61. They are also used by the huntsmen in the lower border of pl. 7. We must assume that such clubs were made from rough pieces of wood, but it is not impossible that some had a heavy metal

Fig. 19 Axe-head from London (British Museum).

225

head.[313] William is depicted holding a club at Hastings (pls. 54, 57 and 68), whereas Harold (pl. 56) is armed with sword and spear. William's club is clearly different from the sceptre carried by Harold and Edward in civil scenes, but again must be taken as a baton of office, perhaps even as a mace *sensu strictu.*

While it must be realized that the Tapestry does not accurately portray either sieges or battles, it is remarkable in providing a vivid evocation of the first recorded major cavalry action in the north. The heavy saddles, long stirrup leathers, the spurs, the couched lance and the kite-shaped shield, all reflect the equipment of a new and disciplined type of soldier. Whilst the Tapestry does not tell us a great deal about either the discipline or the tactics of the armies, it is possible to glimpse some of the practicalities of warfare. We are not presented with many of the levied force of the English. Like the tenth-century poet of *The Battle of Maldon*,[314] we see warfare through the eyes of the people fighting for their chief or king at the highest levels, to whom the foot soldiers were, with the exception of the episode in pls. 66–67, a mere rabble, to be seen off at the end of the story or confined like the Norman archer foot-soldiers to the lower border, literally footnotes to the main story.

As a pendant to this section it is worth commenting briefly on the royal attributes shown in the Tapestry. It has already been pointed out that the king sitting in majesty is in many cases formulaic: he sits on a folding stool in a manner familiar from the late Carolingian period onwards. Edward sits in the Tapestry as he is portrayed on his seal,[315] with splayed legs, as does Harold in his presentation scene as king (pl. 31). Like Edward on his seal, Harold holds orb and sceptre, sitting in majesty as did the Frankish kings and emperors in manuscript and in more official media.[316] The crown is also formulaic: it first appears in an English context on the dedication page of the Corpus Christi Bede (Cambridge, Corpus Christi College, MS 183),[317] which was probably made before 934. The crown here has three upright elements terminating in balls, which have developed by the time they appear in the Tapestry into three trefoils (e.g. pl. 31), paralleling the three upright elements seen in many of the representations of Continental crowns quoted above. No English regalia of this period survives – all that remains are pictures – but we must assume that the Tapestry when portraying regalia, as when portraying so many other things, is dealing in formulae.

Ships

Sea travel is one of the dominant features of the Bayeux Tapestry. The designer seems to have delighted in the form of ships which took passage between England and Normandy and, as no physical remains of ships survive in either England or Normandy to enlarge our experience of eleventh-century

shipping in the Channel, the Tapestry has always been used as the chief basis for discussion or description of shipping in these waters at this period. Once again, the problem of the artist's vision must be considered. Had he seen any ships of this type? Had he indeed even seen a ship of *any* type? There is a fluency about the ships' lines which might suggest that he had, but whether he deliberately differentiated between English and Norman ships on the basis of verbal description is difficult to say. But he did differentiate in one feature, for all the ships used by Harold and the English – with the exception of the ship which brought the news of Harold's accession to William (pl. 33) – have the central portion of the gunwale plank missing. The same detail is even seen on the ships' boat in pl. 5 but is not seen on the Norman ships built by William for the invasion of England. In every other respect, apart from some minor details, as for example the occasional absence of oar-holes, the ships are similar.

In practically every way the ships conform to the type of square-rigged vessel generally familiar from Scandinavian finds of the Viking Age, with rising prow and stern, sometimes embellished with a figurehead and with steering oar on the starboard side.[318] Interesting details include kedging or poling off (pl. 4), the use of oars (pl. 4), anchor (pl. 6), mooring lines (pls. 6 and 37), shields to protect the people in the boat from spray (pl. 6), holes in the stem post to take mooring line (pl. 37) and so on. There is, however, no doubt that the ships are formulaic: in the words of Alan Binns, 'to go as far as to use the tapestry as evidence of asymmetrical hulls, goose-winged sails and other interesting speculations about the detail of Viking ships in the north seems to me to go far beyond what such a document deserves or will support'.[319] Thus it might be possible to see the English ships with the broken line of their gunwale and their oar-holes fore and aft as reflecting the Danish ships of the early eleventh century found at Skuldelev in Roskilde Fjord, where the oar-holes are similarly positioned above decking fore and aft, leaving the space amidships free for cargo.[320] In the same way, the broken line in the gunwale is clearly seen on two of the ships' boats from the Norwegian Gokstad burial,[321] thus accurately paralleling the ship's boat in the Tapestry (pl. 5). We must, however, be careful not to read too much into these parallels.

It is, however, worth considering the generalities of nautical history revealed by the Tapestry. First the Tapestry is explicit that 'William ordered ships to be built'. This so reflects the Scandinavian pattern of offensive warfare as to be more than coincidental. The Scandinavian *leiðangr* was an obligation laid by a king on his coastal provinces to build ships and provide armed men for offensive expeditions and for defence at home. It is enshrined in eleventh- and twelfth-century sources, but clearly has earlier origins.[322] The subject is full of pitfalls but the fact of *leiðangr* exists and, although it altered to suit the king and period, *leiðangr* certainly included as a major element the obligation to furnish the king with a ship as part of military service. Although there are traces of a similar system in England,[323] it would seem likely that William's right to order ships to be built rested on customs imported by his Scandinavian forebears. The size of William's invasion fleet was not necessarily enormous. If, as modern authorities suggest, the army consisted of seven thousand men, these could be accommodated, on the basis of the size of the Scandinavian levy,[324] in between a hundred and a hundred and fifty ships. William's own ship is distinguished from those of his followers as being a great ship (*magno navigo*), perhaps in contrast to the levy ships, which were built quickly and presumably had less refinement. The levy ships were apparently built specifically for the campaign to a convenient and uniform size so that they would have the same sailing capacity – thus limiting the stragglers and allowing for a massive landing at one place. This might be denied in pl. 36 where the ships are of varying sizes, but if Scandinavian levy models were followed, ships of specific dimensions would have been commanded by the duke.

The Tapestry shows the vessels being loaded with food and weapons, and great play is made (pls. 41–43) of the presence of horses on the ships. Bertil Almgren has drawn attention to the ease of landing horses from shallow-drafted Scandinavian ships of the Viking Age and has used the Bayeux Tapestry as supporting evidence.[325] The point of this argument is that it is easier to embark or disembark horses from a ship which draws little water, can be beached and, when so beached, tilts onto its side, than from a higher-sided vessel. The step to be taken in these circumstances by that ill-designed beast, the horse, would only be some 60 cm. Whether Almgren is right or not in his assumptions concerning Viking Age horse transport, it is clear that the Normans made a practice of it. This is the first pictorial evidence of

transport of horses by water in western Europe, although there is reference in literature at an earlier period.[326] The number of horses brought over by the Normans must have been fairly small by comparison with the number of foot soldiers, maybe two or three hundred – two or three horses to each ship.

The ships in the Bayeux Tapestry are not paralleled in manuscript art, although the Anglo-Saxon illustrator of the Bible was sometimes fascinated by Noah's ark, a vessel occasionally portrayed with rising stem and stern posts terminating in fantastic animal-heads.[327] Other pictorial representations, as for example those scratched on a wooden plank from eleventh- or twelfth-century Dublin,[328] on a whetstone from the early Viking Age from Löddeköpinge, Sweden,[329] or on twelfth- and thirteenth-century pieces of wood from Bergen, Norway,[330] are too far away in space, time or artistic achievement to provide useful parallels. Perhaps the best comparison is to be found in literature, in the early eleventh-century *Encomium Emmae Reginae:*

When at length they were all gathered, they went on board the tall ships, having picked out by observation each man his own leader on the brazen prows. On one side lions moulded in gold were to be seen on the ships, on the other birds on the tops of the masts indicated by their movements the winds as they blew, or dragons of various kinds poured fire from their nostrils. Here there were glittering men of solid gold or silver nearly comparable to live ones, there bulls with necks raised high and legs outstretched were fashioned leaping and roaring like live ones. One might see dolphins moulded in electrum, and centaurs in the same metal, recalling the ancient fable. In addition, I might describe to you many examples of the same sort of modelling, if the names of the monsters which were there fashioned were known to me. But why should I not dwell upon the sides of the ships, which were not only painted with ornate colours, but were covered with gold and silver figures? The royal vessel excelled the others in beauty as much as the king preceded the soldiers in the honour of his proper dignity, concerning which it is better that I be silent than that I speak inadequately. Placing their confidence in such a fleet, when the signal was suddenly given, they set out gladly, and, as they had been ordered, placed themselves round about the royal vessel with level prows, some in front and some behind. The blue water, smitten by many oars, might be seen foaming far and wide, and the sunlight cast back in the gleam of metal, spread a double radiance in the air.[331]

Notes

1 Anglo-Saxon Chronicle (D), *sub anno* 1066.

2 C. Stothard, 'Some observations on the Bayeux Tapestry', *Archaeologia*, xix (1821), 184. (The drawings were published in *Vetusta Monumenta*, vi, 1819.)

3 B. de Montfaucon, *Les monuments de la monarchie française*, i, Paris 1729, pl. XXXV.

4 A. Jubinal and V. Sansonetti, *Les anciens tapisseries historiques . . .*, Paris 1838. (I have a suspicion that Sansonetti used Stothard as his model for much of his work; in only one place have I not found a repetition of Stothard's slips in Sansonetti – the spur on pl. 56 is not in Stothard but is in Sansonetti.) It is not without psychological interest that the alleged forger of the Piltdown Skull, Charles Dawson, wrote on the early restoration: C. Dawson, 'The Bayeux Tapestry in the hands of "Restorers" and how it has fared', *The Antiquary*, xliii (1907), 253–8 and 288–92.

5 These measurements were taken by the Sous-Direction des Monuments Historiques to whom I am indebted for permission to quote them. The seven pieces measure in order: 13.65m, 13.75m, 8.35m, 7.75m, 6.60m, 7.15m, 5.25m, according to S. Bertrand, *La tapisserie de Bayeux et la manière de vivre au onzième siècle*, n.p. 1966, 24. These latter measurements were taken before the remounting of the Tapestry in 1983 and are therefore almost certainly in need of revision.

6 The best detailed discussion of the technical aspects of the Tapestry (before it was cleaned) is to be found in Bertrand, *op. cit.* in note 5. With regard to the colour of the linen my judgment depends on the examination in daylight of a fragment of the Tapestry (*ibid.*, pl. at p. 32) which was removed in the 1820s.

7 The method of stitching is reproduced, slightly inaccurately, in M. Rud, *La Tapisserie de Bayeux*, 2nd ed., Bayeux 1983, 12.

8 J. Lang, 'Fine measurement analysis of Viking Age ornament', *Tredie tværfaglige Vikingesymposium*, København 1984, 37–57, and *idem*, 'The compilation of design in colonial Viking sculpture', *Universitetets Oldsaksamling Skrifter*, v (1984), 125–36. D.M. Wilson, *Anglo-Saxon Art from the Seventh Century to the Norman Conquest*, London 1984, 38ff.

9 Much of the historical work on the Tapestry was carried out by Mlle Simone Bertrand, who published her results *op. cit.* in note 5. Much of this section relies on her work. I have not checked all her sources. See also her chapter in F. Stenton (ed.), *The Bayeux Tapestry*, 2nd ed., London 1965, 88–97. A reasonably complete bibliography of the Tapestry is J.J. Marquet de Vasselot and R.-A. Weigert, *Bibliographie de la tapisserie, des tapis et de la broderie en France*, Paris 1935, 288ff. For later bibliographies see O.K. Werckmeister, 'The political ideology of the Bayeux Tapestry', *Studi Medievali*, xvii (1976), 590–95 and an unpublished typescript, N. Moore, *Bibliographie: tenture dite Tapisserie de la Reine Mathilde*, n.d. (deposited in the Society of Antiquaries of London).

10 *Item. une tente tres longue + estroute de telle a broderie de ymages + escpteaulx faisons repṅtoṅ du conquest d angleterre. laquelle est tendue ēniron la nef de l eglē le jour + par les octaves des reliques.* Bertrand, *op. cit.* in note 5, p. 19.

11 Hudson Gurney, 'Observations on the Bayeux Tapestry', *Archaeologia*, xviii (1817), 359. An unlikely looking drawing of the machine is published in C. Dawson, *op. cit.* in note 4, p. 254.

12 Stothard, *op. cit.* in note 2, p. 184.

13 Published in *Vetusta Monumenta*, vi (1835). A coloured version of this complete engraving, preserved in the Society of Antiquaries of London, was probably Stothard's working copy and was exhibited by the Arts Council in 1984 (*English Romanesque Art 1066-1200*, London 1984, no. 551a).

14 Quoted by F.R. Fowke, *The Bayeux Tapestry Reproduced in Autotype Plates*, London 1875, 8.

15 A photograph of this exhibition appears in Dawson, *op. cit.* in note 4, p. 255.

16 Fowke, *op. cit.* in note 14. A half-scale, rolled and coloured copy of Dossetter's series of photographs is deposited in the municipal library at Bayeux. Another is in the Victoria and Albert Museum. This latter formed the basis for the invaluable King Penguin book on the Tapestry by Eric Maclagan (*The Bayeux Tapestry*, Harmondsworth 1943).

17 F. Barlow, *Edward the Confessor*, London 1970, is the only biography. See also F. Barlow, *The Norman Conquest and Beyond*, London 1982.

18 A convenient portrait of Harold is given by H.R. Loyn, *Harold, Son of Godwin*, Bexhill-on-Sea 1966.

19 *Vita Ædwardi Regis* (ed. F. Barlow), London 1962, 30.

20 D.C. Douglas, *William the Conqueror*, London 1964, is a masterly biography.

21 Perhaps the most important and remarkable discussion of the authority of the Tapestry is N.P. Brooks and H.E. Walker, 'The authority and interpretation of the Bayeux Tapestry', *Proceedings of the Battle Conference of Anglo-Norman Studies*, i (1978), (ed. R.A. Brown), Ipswich 1979, 1–34.

22 D.C. Douglas and G.W. Greenaway, *English Historical Documents 1042–1189*, 2nd ed., London 1981, 247 (Referred to as *EHD*).

23 See above, p. 9.

24 H.R. Loyn, *The Norman Conquest*, 3rd ed., London 1982, 91.

25 Guillaume de Jumièges, *Gesta Normannorum Ducum* (ed. J. Marx), Rouen, 1914. For translation see R.A. Brown, *The Norman Conquest*, London 1984 (Documents of Medieval History 5), 3–15. The text is complicated; see E.M.C. van Houts, 'The *Gesta Normannorum Ducum*: a history without an end', *Proceedings of the Battle Conference of Anglo-Norman Studies*, iii (1980), 106–18.

26 R. Foreville (ed.), *Histoire de Guillaume le Conquérant*, Paris 1952. For translation see Brown, *op. cit.* in note 25, pp. 17–41.

27 R. Drögereit, 'Bemerkungen zum Bayeux-Teppich', *Mitteilungen des Instituts für österreichische Geschichtsforschung*, lxxx (1962), 257–93.

28 *Op. cit.* in note 24, p. 9.

29 *Op. cit.* in note 21, p. 5.

30 R.H.C. Davis, 'William of Poitiers and his *History of William the Conqueror*', *The Writing of History in the Middle Ages* (ed. R.H.C. Davis and J.M. Wallace-Hadrill), Oxford 1981, 74.

31 *Op. cit.* in note 19. For summary of the *Vita* as a source, see Brown, *op. cit.* in note 25, pp. 80–82.

32 No satisfactory modern edition of this has been published; see *EHD*, 215, for references to the old editions and for a

translation. For references to recent criticism see Brown, *op. cit.* in note 25, p. 52.

33 R.H.C. Davis, 'The *Carmen de Hastingæ Proelio*', *English Historical Review*, lxvii (1978), 241–61.

34 Stenton, *op. cit.* in note 9, pp. 189ff.

35 The first part of this word is not illustrated in de Montfaucon, *op. cit.* in note 3; the spelling should therefore be treated with caution.

36 I have hesitated to translate this word as 'leader'. Christine Fell has pointed out to me that *ealdorman* is translated as *dux* for example by Æthelweard (A. Campbell, ed., The *Chronicle of Æthelweard*, London 1962), *passim*). The indefinite article makes literal sense, but I would be happy to omit it.

37 The name is a label and not part of the running text.

38 There is no sign of a suspension mark for the *ur* termination on the Tapestry.

39 I have treated this name separately as a label – not as part of the running text.

40 With great reluctance I translate this simply. Cox would render it as 'the old fortification of Hastings', cf. B. Cox, 'The place-names of the earliest English records', *Journal of the English Place-name Society*, 8 (1975–6), 48. The form *Hestingaceastra* is recorded elsewhere as the name for Hastings, cf. *Microfiche Concordance to Old English*, Toronto, *s.v.* 'Hæstingaceastra' and R.E. Latham, *Dictionary of Medieval Latin from British Sources*, London, *s.v.* 'castellum'. See also pp. 188-9. The epexegetic *ceaster* has the same kind of function as 'the city of' in modern forms such as 'the city of Manchester'.

41 This reconstruction of the name is hallowed by tradition. It seems likely that the man portrayed is Eustace of Boulogne who certainly took part in the battle.

42 The sources are ambiguous about this date (see p. 197). I prefer the spring of 1064, as travelling was not a winter activity.

43 Brown, *op. cit.* in note 25, p. 171.

44 Cf. *Vetusta Monumenta*, vi, pl. 1.

45 de Montfaucon, *op. cit.* in note 3, pl. xxxv.

46 W. Stubbs (ed.), Willelmi Malmesbriensis Monachi, *De Gestis Regum Anglorum*, i, 1889, 279 (Chronicles and Memorials of Great Britain and Ireland).

47 *Domesday Book, Sussex*, 6.1-4, 12.33, 12.42, *Hampshire*, 5.1. For a discussion of

Bosham, see R. Gem in *The Archaeological Journal*, cxlii (1985), forthcoming.

48 B. Hougen, 'Et anglo-nordisk drikkehorn fra Holland', *Viking*, iii (1939), 115–28.

49 M. Müller-Wille, 'Das Schiffsgrab von der Ile de Groix (Bretagne) . . .', *Berichte über die Ausgrabungen in Haithabu*, xii (1978), fig. 3:9.

50 A.W. Brögger and H. Shetelig, *The Viking Ships, their ancestry and evolution*, 2nd ed. 1971, 41. R. L. S Bruce-Mitford (ed. A.C. Evans), *The Sutton Hoo Ship-Burial*, iii, London 1983, 316ff.

51 For full (if optimistic) description of these fables see L. Herrmann, *Les Fables antiques de la broderie de Bayeux*, Bruxelles 1964 (Collection Latomus lxix), 19–23.

52 *EDH*, ii, 229 and 231.

53 J. Graham-Campbell, *Viking Artefacts*, London 1980, 282: for other parallels see sources quoted there.

54 A point well made by R.A. Brown, *The Normans and the Norman Conquest*, London 1969, 12.

55 Herrmann, *op. cit.* in note 51, p. 28.

56 Stenton *op. cit.* in note 9, p. 176.

57 Stenton, *op. cit.* in note 9, pp. 24n and 177, cf. also R. Lejeune, 'Turold dans le tapisserie de Bayeux', *Mélanges offerts à René Crozet*, i (ed. P. Gallais and Y.-J. Riou), Poitiers 1966, 419–25. But for the contrary view cf. Brooks and Walker, *op. cit.* in note 21, pp. 8 and 22. I have not seen P.E. Bennett, 'Encore Turold dans la tapisserie de Bayeux', *Annales de Normandie*, xxx (1980), 3–13.

58 *EHD*, ii, 257. Cf. the representation of artists as smaller figures in St Dunstan's Classbook (Bodleian Library, Auct. F. 4. 32) and Eadui in the Eadui Psalter (British Library, Arundel MSS 155), in *The Golden Age of Anglo-Saxon Art, 966–1066* (ed. J. Backhouse, D.H. Turner and L. Webster), London 1984, nos. 31 and 57.

59 C.A. Morris, *Anglo-Saxon and medieval woodworking crafts. The manufacture and use of domestic and utilitarian wooden artifacts in the British Isles 400–1500 A.D.*, Cambridge (Dissertation) 1984, fig. 92.

60 D.M. Wilson, *Anglo-Saxon Art from the Seventh Century to the Norman Conquest*, London 1984, pl. 136.

61 W.A. Seaby and P. Woodfield, 'Viking stirrups from England and their background', *Medieval Archaeology*, xxiv (1980), fig. 9.

62 Herrmann, *op. cit.* in note 51, pp. 30–32, but see also A. Goldschmidt, *An Early Manuscript of the Aesop Fables of Avianus and Related Manuscripts,*

Princeton 1947, 48f.

63 Cf., for example, M. Rickert, *Painting in Britain, the Middle Ages*, 2nd ed., Harmondsworth 1964, pls. 34a and b.

64 Foreville, *op. cit.* in note 26, p. 102.

65 A.W. Brögger and H. Shetelig, *Osebergfundet*, ii, Oslo 1928, figs. 26–8. For later chairs with animal-headed posts, see *ibid.*, figs. 56–63.

66 Herrmann, *op. cit.* in note 51, p. 33.

67 *Ibid.*, p. 31.

68 J.B. McNulty, 'The Lady Aelfgyva in the Bayeux Tapestry', *Speculum*, lv (1980), 659–68.

69 F. Wormald, *The Benedictional of St Ethelwold*, London 1959, pl. 6.

70 Stenton, *op. cit.* in note 9, pp. 178–9.

71 Cf. Brooks and Walker, *op. cit.* in note 21, p. 3.

72 C.R. Dodwell and P.C. Clemoes, *The Old English Illustrated Hexateuch*, Copenhagen 1974, fol. 141v (Early English MSS in facsimile, xviii).

73 Foreville, *op. cit.* in note 26, pp. 102ff.

74 Cf. P.E. Lasko, *Ars Sacra 800–1200*, Harmondsworth 1972, pls. 12, 184, 209, 210, 252 and 257.

75 Herrmann, *op. cit.* in note 51, p. 44.

76 Another interpretation is given *ibid.*, p. 45.

77 Brooks and Walker, *op. cit.* in note 21, p. 11.

78 E.g. *ibid.*, p. 21.

79 Dodwell and Clemoes, *op. cit.* in note 72, fols. 10v, 11v, 12r and *passim*.

80 *Ibid.*, fol. 27v.

81 Stenton, *op. cit.* in note 9, p. 181.

82 *Ibid.*, p. 17.

83 Brown, *op. cit.* in note 25, p. 26.

84 *Op. cit.* in note 9, pp. 17f. Cf. also *EHD*, 271.

85 Herrmann, *op. cit.* in note 51, p. 46.

86 D.M. Wilson (ed.), *The Archaeology of Anglo-Saxon England*, London 1976, fig. 6.1a.

87 *Ibid.*, fig. 6.1h.

88 *Ibid.*, fig. 6.1g.

89 *Ibid.*, fig. 6.2a and b.

90 O. Olsen and O. Crumlin-Petersen, 'The

Skuldelev ships', *Acta Archaeologica,* xxxviii (1967), 122 and fig. 44. For launching of boats see E. Heinsius, 'Der Bildteppich von Bayeux als Quelle für die Seemannschaft der Wikingerzeit', *Vorzeit,* 1966, 4f.

91 J.A. Giles, *Scriptores Rerum Gestarum Willhelmi Conquestoris,* London 1845, 21–2.

92 Dodwell and Clemoes, *op. cit.* in note 72, fol. 66r.

93 E. Temple, *Anglo-Saxon Manuscripts 900–1066,* London 1976, pl. 199.

94 *Berichte über die Ausgrabungen in Haithabu,* xvi (1981), fig. 23b.

95 Foreville, *op. cit.* in note 26, p. 168.

96 R. Cleasby and G. Vigfusson, *An Icelandic-English Dictionary,* Oxford 1874, *s.v.* 'aktaumar'.

97 Translation by Brown, *op. cit.* in note 25, p. 29.

98 *Ibid., loc. cit.*

99 Stenton, *op. cit.* in note 9, p. 32.

100 For most recent commentary see Brooks and Walker, *op. cit.* in note 21, pp. 8 and 193.

101 C.R. Dodwell, 'L'originalité iconographique de plusieurs illustrations anglo-saxonnes de l'Ancien Testament', *Cahiers de civilisation médiévale,* xiv (1971), fig. 22.

102 L.H. Loomis, 'The table of the Last Supper in religious and secular iconography', *Art Studies,* v (1927), 71–88; Brooks and Walker, *op. cit.* in note 21, pp. 15f.

103 D.M. Wilson, *The Anglo-Saxons,* 3rd ed., Harmondsworth 1981, fig. 14.

104 E.g. Dodwell and Clemoes, *op. cit.* in note 72, fol. 37r.

105 Morris, *op. cit.* in note 59, A56–62.

106 Brøgger and Shetelig, *op. cit.* in note 65, pl. xvii.

107 Foreville, *op. cit.* in note 26, p. 180.

108 *Op. cit.* in note 3, ii, pl. VI.

109 Herrmann, *op. cit.* in note 51, p. 49.

110 Herrmann, *ibid.,* p. 50, argues that this is the story of the young man and the prostitute.

111 *Ibid.,* p. 51.

112 For references see Brooks and Walker, *op. cit.* in note 21, p. 193n.

113 R.A. Brown, 'The Battle of Hastings', *Proceedings of the Battle Conference of Anglo-Norman Studies,* iii (ed. R.A. Brown), Bury St Edmunds 1981, 8ff. and sources quoted.

114 Herrmann, *op. cit.* in note 51, pp. 52ff.

115 *EHD,* 239.

116 Herrmann, *op. cit.* in note 51, pp. 55f.

117 Dodwell and Clemoes, *op. cit.* in note 72, fol. 24v ff.

118 Wilson, *op. cit.* in note 60, pl. 34.

119 *Op. cit.* in note 21, p. 32.

120 Brown, *op. cit.* in note 113, pp. 18ff. Cf. also [G.H. White] 'The Battle of Hastings and the death of Harold', *The Complete Peerage,* xii,i, London 1953, Appendix L, p. 42.

121 *Op. cit.* in note 3, pl. viii.

122 Foreville, *op. cit.* in note 26, p. 194.

123 Translation by Brown, *op. cit.* in note 25, p. 32.

124 *Op. cit.* in note 21, pp. 23ff.

125 C.H. Gibbs-Smith, 'The death of Harold at the Battle of Hastings', *History Today,* x (1960), 188–91.

126 D. Bernstein, 'The blinding of Harold and the meaning of the Bayeux Tapestry', *Anglo-Norman Studies,* v (ed. R.A. Brown), Bury St Edmunds 1982.

127 De Montfaucon, *op. cit.* in note 3, pl. ix; *Vetusta Monumenta,* vi (1819), pl. XVI.

128 M. Rule (ed.), *Historia novorum in Anglia,* London 1884 (Rolls Series), 6–8.

129 See Stenton, *op. cit.* in note 9, p. 175. See also D.C. Douglas, *Time and the Hour,* London 1977, 151ff.

130 Anglo-Saxon Chronicle (C and D) *s.a.* 1065.

131 The *Vita Ædwardi* twice points to the long-standing relationship between the English and the counts of Flanders: Barlow, *op. cit.* in note 19, pp. 22 and 54.

132 Brooks and Walker, *op. cit.* in note 21, p. 13.

133 *Vide* Douglas, *op. cit.* in note 20, pp. 178–9, and sources there cited.

134 Translation adapted with minor emendation from Brown, *op. cit.* in note 25, p. 23.

135 *Op. cit.* in note 9, p. 16.

136 Barlow, *op. cit.* in note 19, p. 80.

137 Anglo-Saxon Chronicle (C), *s.a.* 1066.

138 For discussion of these figures, cf. Brown, *op. cit.* in note 54, p. 150n.

139 Brown, *op. cit.* in note 113.

140 *EHD,* 229.

141 *Vetusta Monumenta,* vi (1819), pl. VI. The Holyoke College drawing of the Tapestry, used as an important source in this argument by Brooks and Walker, *op. cit.* in note 21, p. 25, is almost certainly based on Stothard's engravings; although I have not personally had an opportunity to examine the original, the measurements and details coincide.

142 Brooks and Walker, *op. cit.* in note 21, pp. 23ff., and Brown, *op. cit.* in note 113, pp. 17f.

143 W. Stubbs (ed.), Willelmi Malmesbriensis Monachi, *De Gestis Regum Anglorum,* ii, 1889, 303 (Chronicles and Memorials of Great Britain and Ireland).

144 Bernstein, *op. cit.* in note 126, p. 64.

145 *EHD,* 242f. (modified).

146 In Stenton, *op. cit.* in note 9, p. 188.

147 For a discussion of this incident see Brown, *op. cit.* in note 113, pp. 18ff. and quoted sources. For an attempt to locate this incident in relation to the battlefield, see C.H. Lemmon, 'The campaign of 1066', in D. Whitelock *et al., The Norman Conquest,* London 1966, 111f.

148 E.O. Blake (ed.), *Liber Eliensis,* London 1962, ii, 63.

149 A good discussion of the sources is R. Dodwell, *Anglo-Saxon Art, a new perspective,* Manchester 1982, 129ff.

150 *Antiquity,* lviii (1984), 73.

151 Quoted in Dodwell, *op. cit.* in note 149, p. 130.

152 *Ibid.,* 139.

153 P. Abrahams (ed.), *Les oeuvres poétiques de Baudri de Bourgueil,* Paris 1926, 202 (lines 207–12). Abrahams, p. 234, points out that the poet had no intention of giving an exact description of what he had seen.

154 Wilson, *op. cit.* in note 60, pls. 107–9. See also M. Budny and D. Tweddle, 'The Maaseik embroideries', *Anglo-Saxon England,* xiii (1984), 65–96.

155 C.F. Battiscombe (ed.), *The Relics of St Cuthbert,* Oxford 1956, pls. xxlvff.

156 C.M. Kauffmann, *Romanesque Manuscripts 1066–1190,* London 1975, 19.

157 For this see Stenton, *op. cit.* in note 9, p. 33; see also above, p. 12.

158 *Op. cit.* in note 14. Already in 1833 Henry Ellis had pointed to the fact that two of Odo's tenants appear on the Tapestry: *General Introduction to Domesday*, ii, London 1833 (reprinted 1971), 513.

159 In Stenton, *op. cit.* in note 9, p. 33f.

160 C.R. Dodwell, 'The Bayeux Tapestry and the French Secular Epic', *The Burlington Magazine*, cviii (1966), 549–60.

161 T.A. Shippey, *Old English Verse*, London 1972, 175f.

162 *The Battle of Maldon*, ll. 237–42 (ed. D.G. Scragg) Manchester 1981.

163 *Ibid.*

164 English examples listed in M. Wood, *The English Medieval House*, London, new ed. 1981, 45. See also P.A. Rahtz in Wilson, *op. cit.* in note 86, pp. 65ff.

165 *Royal Commission on Historical Monuments England . . . London*, ii (1925), 120ff.

166 M. de Boüard, 'La salle dite de l'Exchiquier au Château de Caen', *Medieval Archaeology*, ix (1965), 64–81.

167 Brooks and Walker, *op. cit.* in note 21, p. 10.

168 R. Lepelley, 'Contribution à l'étude des inscriptions de la tapisserie de Bayeux', *Annales de Normandie*, xlv (1964), 321.

169 M. Förster, 'Zur Geschichte des Reliquienkultus in Altengland', *Sitzungsberichte des Bayerischen Akademie der Wissenschaften* (Phil.-Hist. Abt.), viii (1943), 16–19. Lepelley, *op. cit.* in note 168, *passim*.

170 S. Kraft, *Pictorial Weavings from the Viking Age*, Oslo 1956, and H. Shetelig, *Kunst*, Oslo 1931, 221 (Nordisk Kultur, xxvii) for photograph. See also A. Geijer, *Ur textilkonstens historia*, Lund 1972, 276ff.

171 For references to this later material, Stenton, *op. cit.* in note 9, pp. 48f. and references cited.

172 Cf. Dodwell, *op. cit.* in note 149, pp. 135f. and for Adela's Tapestry, Abrahams, *op. cit.* in note 153, p. 196ff.

173 A. Andersson, *The Art of Scandinavia*, ii, London 1970, 392ff.

174 Backhouse, *et al.*, *op. cit.* in note 58, pp. 133f.

175 *Ibid.*, 133.

176 *English Romanesque Art 1066–1200* (Exhibition Catalogue, Hayward Gallery), London 1984, 150f.

177 Wilson, *op. cit.* in note 60, p. 200.

178 For Lincoln and Bury see G. Zarnecki, *Studies in Romanesque Sculpture*, London 1975, xv.

179 *on denisc ableredum hneccan* (Danish . . . shaven necks). Oxford, Bodleian MS, Hatton 115, published F. Kluge, 'Fragment eines angelsächsischen Briefes', *Englische Studien*, viii (1885), 62–3 . N. Ker, *Catalogue of Manuscripts containing Anglo-Saxon*, Oxford 1957, no. 332, article 15. For the long hair of the English see Dodwell, *op. cit.* in note 149, p. 217 and n.

180 Most conveniently listed in Herrmann, *op. cit.* in note 51. See also Goldschmidt, *op. cit.* in note 62, pp. 48f.

181 E.g. D.M. Wilson, *Anglo-Saxon Ornamental Metalwork, 700–1100, in the British Museum*, London 1964, pl. xvi.

182 In Stenton, *op. cit.* in note 9, p. 30. Cf. C.R. Dodwell and P.C. Clemoes, *op. cit.* in note 72, e.g. fols. 3r, 28r, 30r, 36r and 36v.

183 T.D. Kendrick, *Late Saxon and Viking Art*, London 1949, pl. xxi, 2.

184 Kauffmann, *op. cit.* in note 156, p. 19. For a good selection of Norman illumination, see J.J.G. Alexander, *Norman Illumination at Mont St Michel, 966–1100*, Oxford 1970.

185 Wilson, *op. cit.* in note 181, fig. 5.

186 F. Wormald, *Collected Writings*, i, Oxford 1982, pls. 57f.

187 E.g. Wilson, *op. cit.* in note 181, pls. xxxvii, xii, xiii and xxiv, 44.

188 Zarnecki, *op. cit.* in note 178, pl. xviiia.

189 E.g. C.R. Dodwell, *The Canterbury School of Illumination 1066–1200*, Cambridge 1954, pls. 7b, 7c, etc.

190 Dodwell and Clemoes, *op. cit.* in note 72, fol. 41v.

191 *Ibid.*, fols. 40r, 52r and v.

192 *Ibid.*, fol. 13v.

193 Stenton, *op. cit.* in note 9, figs. 4–21.

194 P.E. Schramm, *Die deutschen Kaiser und Könige in Bildern ihrer Zeit*, Berlin 1928, pls. *passim*.

195 F. Wormald, *English Drawings of the Tenth and Eleventh Century*, London 1952, pls. *passim*.

196 Stenton, *op. cit.* in note 9, pp. 32f.

197 *Ibid.*, 30f.

198 Cf. S. Horn Fuglesang, *Some Aspects of the Ringerike Style*, Odense 1980, pls. 69 and 70.

199 *Ibid.*, 75.

200 For illustration of Norman foliage see Alexander, *op. cit.* in note 184, pls. 8ff. For English Romanesque tendrils, see Kauffmann, *op. cit.* in note 156, pls. 1–18.

201 *Op. cit.* in note 149, p. 70ff.; cf. also C. Fell, *Women in Anglo-Saxon England*, London 1984, 42.

202 Brooks and Walker, *op. cit.* in note 21, p. 9.

203 Most recently by M. Parisse, *La tapisserie de Bayeux*, n.p. 1983, 81ff.

204 Bertrand, *op. cit.* in note 5, p. 32.

205 J.M. Backhouse, 'The making of the Harley Psalter', *British Library Journal*, x (1984), 97–113.

206 Cf. most recently Bertrand, *op. cit.* in note 5, 270ff.; R.A. Brown, *English Castles*, 3rd ed., London 1976, 35, 58; H. Hinz, *Motte und Donjon*, Köln 1981, fig. 23; *Archéologie Médiévale*, xi (1981), 35.

207 Cf. Hinz, *op. cit.* in note 206, the caption of fig. 22 and *contra* p. 153.

208 'Colloque de Caen', *Archéologie Médiévale*, xi (1981), 9. Cf. also J. Yver, 'Les châteaux fortes en Normandie jusqu'au milieu du xiie siècle', *Bulletin de la Société des Antiquaires de Normandie*, liii (1955–6), 28–115. A highly critical examination of the evidence suggests that they were not so plentiful as many scholars would postulate, *vide* B. K. Davison, 'Early earthwork castles: a new model', *Chateau Gaillard*, iii (1969), 33–47.

209 For this cf. P. Héliot, 'Sur les résidences princières bâties en France du Xe au XIIe siècle', *Le Moyen Age*, lxi (1955), 46f.

210 Brown, *op. cit.* in note 206, 50f.

211 M. Jones, 'The defence of medieval Brittany . . .', *The Archaeological Journal*, cxxxviii (1981), 157f.

212 Brown, *op. cit.* in note 206, 43ff.

213 See J. Bosworth and T.N. Toller, *An Anglo-Saxon Dictionary (and supplement)*, *s.v.* 'castel'. For this interpretation of Dover cf. R.A. Brown, 'The Norman conquest and the genesis of English castles', *Chateau Gaillard*, iii (1969), 10f.

214 P.E. Curnow and F.H. Thompson, 'Excavations at Richard's Castle, Herefordshire (1962–1964)', *Journal of the British Archaeological Association*, 3rd ser. xxxii (1969), 105–27.

215 G. Beresford, 'Goltho manor, Lincolnshire, the buildings and their surrounding defences c.850–1150', *Proceedings of the Battle Conference of Anglo-Norman Studies*, iv (1981) (ed. R.A. Brown), 13–36. The case against mottes in England before the Conquest is cogently argued by Davison, *op. cit.* in note 208.

216 Hinz, *op. cit.* in note 206, p. 35; P.A. Barker and K.J. Barton, 'Excavations at Hastings Castle, 1968', *The Archaeological Journal*, cxxxiv (1977), 83.

217 *Ibid.*

218 For Dinan, see *Congrès archéologique de France*, cvii (1950), 172.

219 Mont-Dol, a granite outcrop 3 km north-west of the town is traditionally, on no evidence at all, taken to be the site of the motte illustrated in the Bayeux Tapestry.

220 P.V. Addyman and J. Priestley, 'Baile Hill, York', *The Archaeological Journal*, cxxxiv (1977), 124.

221 In Stenton, *op. cit.* in note 9, p. 82 for references.

222 This capital is now displayed in the Jewel House, Westminster.

223 B. Hope-Taylor, 'The excavation of a motte at Abinger, Surrey', *The Archaeological Journal*, cvii (1950), 15–43.

224 *Op. cit.* in note 213, p. 13.

225 H. Hinz, 'Zu zwei Darstellungen auf dem Teppich von Bayeux', *Chateau Gaillard*, vi (1973), 110.

226 H.M. Colvin (ed.), *The History of the King's Works*, i, London 1963, 45ff.

227 P.A. Rahtz, *The Saxon and Medieval Palaces at Cheddar*, Oxford 1979 (BAR, British Series 65), 57ff.

228 J.H. Williams, 'From "palace" to "town": Northampton and urban origins', *Anglo-Saxon England*, xiii (1984), 113–36. I have yet to be convinced of this very early dating. Could this hall be of tenth-century date?

229 Stenton, *op. cit.* in note 9, p. 80.

230 Anglo-Saxon Chronicle, *s.a.* 1086.

231 In Stenton, *op. cit.* in note 9, p. 80.

232 *Ibid.*, p. 83.

233 *Ibid.*, *loc. cit.*

234 M. Wood, *Norman Domestic Architecture*, London 1974, *passim*.

235 Rahtz, *op. cit.* in note 227, fig. 32. B.K. Davison, 'Excavations at Sulgrave, Northamptonshire 1960–76', *The Archaeological Journal*, cxxxiv (1977), 105–14.

236 E.g. Wood, *op. cit.* in note 234, and *idem*, *op. cit.* in note 164, 1–15.

237 Cf. R. Hall, *The Viking Dig*, London 1984, 71.

238 U.T. Holmes, 'The houses of the Bayeux Tapestry', *Speculum*, xxxiv (1959), 183.

239 Parisse, *op. cit.* in note 203, p. 115.

240 E. Fernie, *The Architecture of the Anglo-Saxons*, London 1983, 22.

241 For Bosham, see H.M. and J. Taylor, *Anglo-Saxon Architecture*, Cambridge 1965, 81–4 and pls. 397–9. Most scholars would now deny the Taylors' interpretation of the church: cf. R.D.H. Gem, *The Archaeological Journal*, cxlii (1985), forthcoming.

242 In Stenton, *op. cit.* in note 9, p. 79.

243 The best account of this building is R.D.H. Gem, 'The Romanesque rebuilding of Westminster Abbey', *Proceedings of the Battle Congress of Anglo-Norman Studies*, iii (ed. R.A. Brown), Bury St Edmunds 1981, 33–60, with its references.

244 *Ibid.*, p. 36.

245 *Ibid.*, p. 37.

246 See above, p. 178.

247 E.g. Dodwell and Clemoes, *op. cit.* in note 72, fol. 27v.

248 Bruce-Mitford, *op. cit.* in note 50, pp. 415f.

249 *Ibid.*, p. 888. Cf. European parallels quoted.

250 Temple, *op. cit.* in note 93, pl. 148.

251 Bosworth and Toller, *op. cit.* in note 213, *s.v.* 'pyle'.

252 Temple, *op. cit.* in note 93, pls. 132 and *passim*.

253 E.g. *ibid.*, pls. 87, 148.

254 Brøgger and Shetelig, *op. cit.* in note 65, pp. 81ff.

255 Dodwell and Clemoes, *op. cit.* in note 72, fol. 55r.

256 *Ibid.*, fols. 10v, 11v and *passim*.

257 Dodwell, *op. cit.* in note 149, 162ff. and pl. 39.

258 For various medieval openings of the tomb see Barlow, *op. cit.* in note 17, p. 254.

259 Dodwell, *op. cit.* in note 101, figs. 21–22.

260 See, for example, A. MacGregor, *Anglo-Scandinavian Finds from Lloyds Bank, Pavement and Other Sites*, York 1982 (The archaeology of York, xvii), 138ff.

261 In Stenton, *op. cit.* in note 9, p. 72.

262 Wilson, *op. cit.* in note 181, pp. 52f.

263 Battiscombe, *loc. cit.* in note 155.

264 Noted by Fell, *op. cit.* in note 201, figs. 16 and 22.

265 In Stenton, *op. cit.* in note 9, pp. 56–69.

266 See N.P. Brooks, 'Arms, status and warfare in Late-Saxon England', *Ethelred the Unready* (ed. D. Hill), Oxford 1978, 81 (BAR, British Series lix).

267 Stenton, *op. cit.* in note 9, fig. 26.

268 G. Engelhardt, *Vimose Fundet*, København 1869, 12 and pl. 4. For ninth- and tenth-century examples, see those from Birka, Sweden, in Stenton, *op. cit.* in note 9, pl. 37, and from Gjermundbu, Norway, in S. Grieg, *Gjermundbufunnet*, Oslo 1947, pl. iv (Norske Oldfunn, viii).

269 R.L.S. Bruce-Mitford, *The Sutton Hoo Ship-Burial*, ii, London 1978, 237.

270 D. Tweddle, 'The Coppergate Helmet', *Fornvännen*, 1983, 105–12, and *idem*, *The Coppergate Helmet*, York 1984.

271 Wilson, *op. cit.* in note 60, pls. 34 and 36.

272 Cf. same scene in British Library, Harley 603, fol. 73; G.F. Laking, *A Record of European Arms and Armour*, i, London 1920, fig. 31.

273 Cf., for example, *English Romanesque Art 1066–1200*, London 1984, 57, 103, 110; Stenton *op. cit.* in note 9, fig. 32; E. Carus-Wilson, 'Haubergel: a medieval textile conundrum', *Medieval Archaeology*, xiii (1969), pls. xv, xvia and xvii.

274 J. Porcher, *French Miniatures from Illuminated Manuscripts*, London 1960, pl. xxvi. For a good twelfth-century English example from the Winchester Bible, see J. Mann, *Arms and Armour in England*, London 1969, 7.

275 E. von Lenz, *Die Waffensammlung des Grafen S.D. Scheremetew in St Petersburg*, Leipzig 1897, pl. ii, 49.

276 *Op. cit.* in note 21, p. 19.

277 D.J.A. Ross, 'L'originalité de "Turoldus": le maniement de la lance', *Cahiers de civilisation médiévale*, vi (1963), fig. 5.

278 R.L.S. Bruce-Mitford, *Aspects of Anglo-Saxon Archaeology*, London 1974, 223–49.

279 Bruce-Mitford, *op. cit.* in note 269, p. 138–231.

280 *Ibid.*, fig. 178e.

281 D. Hejdová, 'Přilba Zvaná "Svatováclavská"', *Sborník Národního Muzea v Praze*, Ser. A, xviii (1964), 1–106.

282 *Ibid.*, pl. xiiib; Stenton, *op. cit.* in note 9, fig. 33.

283 Hejdová, *op. cit.* in note 281, pl. xiiia.

284 E. von Lenz, 'In Russland gefundene frühmittelalterliche Helme', *Zeitschrift für historische Waffen- und Kostümkunde*, new series i (Beiheft) (1923–5), fig. 12.

285 *Ibid.*, fig. 13.

286 For references see E. Munksgaard, 'A Viking Age smith, his tools and his stock in trade', *Offa*, xli (1984), 87.

287 E.g. G. Galster, *Royal Collection of Coins and Medals, National Museum Copenhagen*, iiic, London 1970, pls. 146, 4077–80 (Sylloge of coins of the British Isles, xv).

288 Cf. for late eleventh-century French example, Porcher, *op. cit.* in note 274, pl. xxvi. English examples can be seen in *English Romanesque Art 1066–1200*, London 1984, 57, 103, 110, 303 and 313. Stenton *op. cit.* in note 9, fig. 32.

289 A. Grabar and C. Nordenfalk, *Early Medieval Painting*, n.p. 1957, 212, 215f.

290 E.g. Dodwell and Clemoes, *op. cit.* in note 72, fol. 24v; I. Gollancz, *The Caedmon Manuscript*, Oxford 1927, 57.

291 For discussion of shields see Wilson, *op. cit.* in note 103, pp. 120ff.

292 Bruce-Mitford, *op. cit.* in note 269, pp. 1–128.

293 Wilson, *op. cit.* in note 60, pl. 34.

294 C.R. Dodwell, *Painting in Europe 800–1200*, Harmondsworth 1971, pls. 48 and 50.

295 E.g. H.R. Ellis Davidson, *The Sword in Anglo-Saxon England*, Oxford 1962, figs. 23–7, 74.

296 E.g. *ibid.*, fig. 70; J. Ypey, 'Einige wikingerzeitliche Schwerter aus den Niederlanden', *Offa*, 41 (1984), 213–25, *passim*.

297 Cf., e.g. M. Swanton, *A Corpus of Pagan Anglo-Saxon Spear-types*, Oxford 1974 (British Archaeological Reports 7).

298 For spearheads of Scandinavian type dated to the eleventh century by their ornament see Horn Fuglesang, *op. cit.* in note 198, 29ff.

299 Cf. G. Bersu and D.M. Wilson, *Three Viking Graves in the Isle of Man*, London 1966 (The Society for Medieval Archaeology, Monograph Series: I), fig. 44 and references cited on p. 76.

300 R.E.M. Wheeler, *London and the Vikings*, London 1927 (London Museum Catalogues: I), fig. 12, 1 and references cited on p. 28.

301 For these tactics cf. Ross, *op. cit.* in note 277, pp. 127–38, and Brown, *op. cit.* in note 54, pp. 12ff.

302 *Ibid.*, p. 200.

303 Line 110, Scragg, *op. cit.* in note 162.

304 Wilson, *op. cit.* in note 60, pl. 34.

305 For a recent summary of arrow finds in northern Europe, see M. Müller-Wille, *Das Bootkammergrab von Haithabu*, Neumünster 1976 (Berichte über die Ausgrabungen in Haithabu, viii), 82f. For arrow-heads of other materials see Graham-Campbell, *op. cit.* in note 53, p. 12.

306 London Museum *Medieval Catalogue*, 3rd impression 1967, 65ff.

307 Müller-Wille, *op. cit.* in note 49, p. 52, figs. 3: 4–7.

308 Graham-Campbell, *op. cit.* in note 53, fig. 266.

309 See P.G. Foote and D.M. Wilson, *The Viking Achievement*, London 1970, 278. For bows in general, see G. Rausing, *The Bow, some notes on its origin and development*, Lund 1967.

310 R. Cramp, *County Durham and Northumberland*, ii, London 1984, pls. 201 and 1133 (The British Academy Corpus of Anglo-Saxon Sculpture, i).

311 *Kulturhistorisk Leksikon for nordisk middelalder*, xx, København 1976, 653.

312 *Op. cit.* in note 54, p. 198.

313 Cf. Graham-Campbell, *op. cit.* in note 53, p. 76. Dating of such heads is often difficult, cf. later examples, N.-K. Liebgott, *Middelalderens Våben*, København 1976, 17.

314 Scragg, *op. cit.* in note 162.

315 Brown, *op. cit.* in note 25, p. 171.

316 Cf. Schramm, *op. cit.* in note 194, *passim*.

317 Wilson, *op. cit.* in note 60, pl. 203.

318 Much has been written concerning Viking ships in recent years. A Binns, *Viking Voyagers*, London 1980, 239f., gives the chief references.

319 *Ibid.*, pp. 64f.

320 Olsen and Crumlin-Pedersen, *op. cit.* in note 90, fig. 44.

321 Brøgger and Shetelig, *op. cit.* in note 50, p. 41.

322 For *lei angr* see P.S. Andersen, *Samlingen av Norge og kristningen av landet*, Bergen, Oslo, Tromsø 1977, (Handbok i Norges historie, ii), 262–73; I. Skovgaard-Petersen, A.E. Christiansen and H. Paludan, *Danmarks Historie: Tiden indtil 1340*, i. København 1977, 194–7 and 251; N. Lund, 'Lid og Leding', *Andet tværfaglige Vikingesymposium*, Aarhus 1983, 23–38. For a slightly broader, but now rather outdated summary, see *Kulturhistorisk Leksikon for nordisk middelalder*, x, København 1963, s.v. 'Leidang'. A summary in English, based on rather late sources, is in Foote and Wilson, *op. cit.* in note 309, pp. 280–2.

323 F.M. Stenton, *Anglo-Saxon England*, 3rd ed., Oxford 1971, 582n.

324 Binns, *op. cit.* in note 318, pp. 62ff., gives some figures but these should be examined critically in relation to the original sources.

325 B. Almgren, 'Vikingatågens höjdpunkt och slut', *Tor*, 1963, 215–50.

326 At Messina in 1064. Cf. J. Beeler, *Warfare in Feudal Europe, 730–1200*, Ithaca and London 1971, 84.

327 E.g. British Library Cotton Claudius B IV, Dodwell and Clemoes, *op. cit.* in note 72, fols. 14r, 14v, 15r, 15v.

328 *Viking and Medieval Dublin*, Dublin 1973 (National Museum of Ireland exhibition catalogue), cover and pl. 11.

329 Graham-Campbell, *op. cit.* in note 53, no. 281.

330 A. Herteig, 'The excavation of Bryggen . . . Bergen', *Medieval Archaeology*, iii (1959), fig. 68.

331 Slightly adapted from A. Campbell (ed.), *Encomium Emmae Reginae*, London 1949, 13 (Camden Series, 3, vol. lxxii).

Index